Martin Pöppel

HEAVEN
AND HELL

Martin Pöppel, 1941

HEAVEN AND HELL

The War Diary
of a
German Paratrooper

MARTIN PÖPPEL
Translated from the German by
Dr Louise Willmot

SPELLMOUNT
Staplehurst

Also published by Spellmount

The Devil's Adjutant: Jochen Peiper, Panzer Leader
Michael Reynolds

The Forgotten Battle: Overloon and the Maas Salient 1944–45
A. Korthals Altes & N. K. C. A. In't Veld

The War North of Rome: June 1944–May 1945
Thomas Brooks

The Battle for Moscow
Colonel Albert Seaton

The Glider Soldiers
Alan Wood

Overlord Coastline: The Major D-Day Locations
Stephen Chicken

The Unforgettable Army: Slim's XIVth Army in Burma
Colonel Michael Hickey

One Family's War
edited by Patrick Mayhew

Tainted Goddesses: Female Film Stars of the Third Reich
Cinzia Romani

The Scottish Regiments 1633–1996
Patrick Mileham

English and Welsh Infantry Regiments
Ray Westlake

The Territorial Battalions
Ray Westlake

The History of British Military Bands – *3 Volumes*
Gordon and Alwyn Turner

Ihr dürft nicht alles zu »eng«
sehen. Das Meiste stamt aus meinen
Tagebüchern und Gefechtsaufzeichnungen,
aber auch Berichte und Erinnerungen
von Euch wurden eingeflochten.
Und die Sprache kann nicht »modern«
sein.
Es sind die Aufzeichnungen eines
damals 18 bis 25jährigen,
der anderes im Kopf hatte, als Poesie.
Daher habe ich ohne
Schnörkel und Scham so geschrieben
wie mir damals zumute war
und ich es aufgezeichnet hatte.

Erinnert Euch:

British Library Cataloging in Publication Data
A catalogue record for this book is available
from the British Library

ISBN 1-873376-64-2

First published in German by
Internationales Kulturdienst, Postf 370226,
8 München 37, Germany

First published in the UK in 1988 by
Spellmount Limited
The Old Rectory
Staplehurst
Kent TN12 0AZ

Printed in the United States

Contents

Military Career and Active Service of Martin Pöppel

1938	Labour Service.
1938	Recruit into 1 Parachute Regiment, 4 Company.
1939	Parachute training in Stendal attached to Regimental Signal Communication Platoon.
10.5.1940	Drop over Holland-Dordrecht, Iron Cross First and Second Class.
	Early promotion to Oberjäger.
June 1940	Drop on Narvik.
	Transfer to Parachute Machine Gun Battn. 7.
20.5.1941	Drop on Rethymnon, Crete.
	Feldwebel attached to Dresden-Klotsche Airborne Training School. Promoted to Leutnant in December.
January 1942	Service on Russian front – Sobakino-Rzhev.
10.7. – 13.8.1943	Service on Sicily – Catania. Oberleutnant.
14.8. – 4.10.1943	Southern Italy.
15.1.1944	Transfer to 6 Parachute Regiment as Company Commander 12 Company.
6.6.1944	Normandy – Carentan.
November 1944	Parachute Weapons School.
Feb./Mar. 1945	Assault Battn. of Parachute Army, Roer, Reichswald, Xanten, Rees on Rhine.
23 March 1945 until March 1946	POW in England

This is how it all began:

Shortly after the Nazis came to power, I transferred from the Catholic boy scouts' organisation *Neudeutschland* (New Germany) to the Hitler Youth and was accepted into its *Jungvolk* section (for boys aged 10-14) on 13th April 1933. A year later I was made a patrol leader, which made me the most senior boy in our little community. On 1st June 1936 I became a 'freshwater sailor', which means that I transferred to the Marine section of the Hitler Youth and passed the marksman's examination at the Reich Shooting School at Obermassfeld in Thuringia.

Consequently, it seemed obvious that I would join the Navy after I left school. But because I was a volunteer and a schoolboy, I would have been forced to serve for four years – which I wasn't prepared to do. Although I really enjoyed the scouting activities in the Hitler Youth, along with the sports and marksmanship, I didn't want to spend four whole years doing it. Instead I reported to the Luftwaffe, as the Neubiberg air base was near where I lived. However, it was the same story there: 'Schoolboy? Then it's four years for you.' So that was out as well, as far as I was concerned. Then whilst I was with the Sport Department of the compulsory Labour Service at Donauwörth, I saw an article in an illustrated magazine about the new paratroops. When I found out more about them, I discovered that I would only have to serve two years with them. That was for me – even though I was a Bavarian lad and would have to travel a long way north for my training. Though I didn't know it yet, I had already shown that I was a suitable candidate for the paratroops during the Labour Service, when my Department Leader came across me in the sentry box, where I was supposed to be on guard, sitting on a spade with a quart of beer in my hand. A bit of spirit, something out of the ordinary was what the paratroops wanted – although I only found that out some time later.

Yes – and then my story really began.

I reported for duty to the 'General Goring' Regiment in Berlin Reinickendorf, and a few days later was among the first years' intake of recruits sent by train to Stendal. At the station we were welcomed by an excruciating version of the song 'All the little birds are here', played by a local band. But perhaps the song wasn't so very far off the mark: we were soon to become eagles, after all.

We marched proudly through the town in our civilian clothes. Since we all knew we had joined a superb elite, we were desperately disappointed to find that our accommodation was only a hutted camp. It made a pretty amusing scene, in fact. There we stood in rough-and-ready formation, whilst in front of us towered giants of men, standing ramrod straight, chests out – just the way Old Fritz used to like them. At 1.72 metres high myself, about 5′ 8″, I felt fairly puny alongside them. After a few rasping orders, I became

Soldier Martin Pöppel
Army Post Office no. 36480
Post Collecting Point Oppeln

in 1 Parachute Regiment (Fallschirmjägerregiment), 1st Battalion, 1 Company, 2 Platoon, 4 Group.

Feldwebel Toschka – one of these giants – was platoon leader. Leutnant Becker, an unusual sight in the paratroops because he was small, was in charge of my section of recruits. Our Company was commanded by Haputman Gericke, another fine figure of a man. Our senior soldier was Gefreite Heitmann, a fine fellow who was easy to recognise because he usually had an enormous plaster on his uniform collar to disguise a persistent boil. Another enormous man was the Sarge, Hauptfeldwebel Zierach. He reigned supreme with his fat punishment book, which he kept jammed between the first and second button on his chest. Sad to say, over the next few weeks he was to note my name in it with distressing regularity. Thank God, we didn't see him often during basic training, but when he arrived there was hell to pay. His sixth sense – which Sergeant Majors have more of than other mortals – recorded everything that went on. Whenever he looked at us poor squirts we started to tremble. But as I say, we didn't see him often. Our Company Commander Gericke wasn't around us much either, and we regarded him as a real god of war.

Our training was unbelievably hard, but basically fair. It passed quickly even if only because we were drilled so hard from morning till night that we never got a moment to think. But after a couple of weeks I knew that there was no way I could be a career soldier. Being forced to keep quiet no matter what, not being permitted to discuss things or defend my point of view – that's not for me.

However, I came to understand that for these two years I would have to be less obstinate than usual. During one of the many punishment drills which so aroused my spirit of resistance, a Pomeranian Oberjäger with a mouth which stretched from ear to ear planted himself in front of me: 'Pöppel, aren't you finished yet?'

Being a fool, I grinned at him and landed myself in more trouble. Running on the spot, marching and falling flat, marching and punishment routines to music – for me at least, they were never-ending. But although I wasn't as big as these fatheads, I could still be damned tough and cussed and I'd never let my spirit be broken.

My best skills were in shooting. I already had a head start here because I'd been something of a marksman during my days in the Hitler Youth, so I soon got a little bit of special leave to compensate me for a few punishment drills. In the hundred metres prone I scored 34 out of 36 possible rings in the silhouette target and I was equally successful with the heavy machine gun, scoring four out of five possible hits. I became the 'poacher', the sharpshooter, my basic skills much improved by the hard training. Naturally, I celebrated my success with sausages and beer.

As part of my training I had to travel to Hanover for the psychological tests for flyers. A great show was made of these, but they were actually quite simple. What little money I possessed had been spent in the city's 'Moulin Rouge' the night before, so I had to spend several hours walking in Hanover before the tests. A few days later, I was sent to the Parachute School in Borstel, for instructions in the static-line back-pack parachute and in the art of packing a parachute correctly.

Suddenly, in March 1939, there was a flurry of excitement. The men were confined to camp, weapons containers were brought to the airfield and we found ourselves helping to load ammunition. The barracks was sealed off, with no one allowed to leave without special permission. Two days later the first platoons left the camp and then the last of the 'Old Men' pushed off as well. Some hundred Ju's, or Junkers aircraft, were due to set off and take our 1 Parachute Regiment for immediate service in Czechoslovakia. At the time, I was bitter that we weren't allowed to take part and I wrote: 'The fact that we 'boys' aren't allowed to go is the biggest load of shit this century, there's only a month to go before we finish training and then we'd have been there. Shit and damnation!' In fact, the planes finally set off next day, at six in the morning. I remember we watched with genuine anger and tears as the machines took off and flew in formation. However, our disappointment was replaced by great enthusiasm when Dr Goebbels made a special radio broadcast to announce that Czechoslovakia had been taken over by the Reich. We were uncritically enthusiastic, proud to be alive in times we regarded as heroic.

The First Parachute Jump

Basic parachute training – rolling backwards and forwards, hanging from the parachute – is finally complete. It's time for our first jump, an experience which we still find it hard to imagine. We are itching to do it at last.

After a week of rain, we wake up to glorious sunshine. Out to the airfield, parachutes on and into the Ju's. Why is it so quiet all of a sudden? The jokes and platitudes tail away and somehow everybody becomes thoughtful. The night before we had talked for ages, and just for fun I made a will. Much later, after I was reported missing in March 1945, my mother found this will and read it. In my youthful frivolity I had simply written 'My last wish, a wife with glasses' ('Mein letzter Wille, eine Frau mit Brille'). When my mother got my case back and read those words, she thought: 'Well, that proves it – the lad is surely still alive!'

The aircraft circles five times, then I find myself by the open hatch, the first man out. Strangely, my anxiety suddenly disappears. Wonderful – I'm out. A little bump as the canopy opens and I float gently down to earth, land and gather up the parachute. I have a fantastic, indescribable feeling of pleasure, mixed with pride that I am now a real paratrooper. I report happily to Oberleutnant Moll: 'Jäger Pöppel, first jump completed without injury!' When the leader of the training unit says that my jump was the best, I'm honestly so happy I could burst. After the six-man and twelve-man jumps have been completed successfully, Hauptmann Kroh takes leave of the successful soldiers.

Regiment Signal Communication Platoon

Either my IQ was higher, or more probably my superior officers had last got sick of me. At any rate, I was sent to the Signal Communication Platoon in room 2. I was only there a few days before moving on to 2 Company barracks to Gefreite Erich (Sascha) Surowka in room 9 – a fine fellow, as you will discover in this book. Unfortunately there were others, for example Oberjäger Schönfeld, who didn't take such a favourable view of me. This clot had it in for me, and reported me simply because of a silly bit of elastic on my training-suit. Then Oberfeldwebel Moser, a sturdy fellow from Swabia, wanted me as a batman. Me of all people, who was hardly capable of keeping my own things in order let alone anyone else's.

The Commander of 1 Parachute Regiment in Stendal-Borstel in 1940 was Oberst
Bruno Bräuer (left). In the centre, Regimental Signal Communications Platoon
leader Oberleutnant Schuller. Right, Hauptmann Prager from II Battalion.

Parachute training in Stendal-Borstel

In Stendal-Borstel barracks. The Regimental Signal Communications Platoon: in front, Feldwebel 'Pipl' Weber; from the left, among others, Feldwebel Mürbe, Oberjäger Erich Sorowka, and Jäger Tröger, Güttler and Eberhard Schäfer.

Paratrooper in full dress uniform.

But he dropped the idea at once when I told him that I would still be studying in my spare time (in fact, apart from girls I hadn't any intention of studying anything). And then there were those little gods, our Lance Corporals, our Gefreite. Wickert discovered me when I was out after lights out – report, leave cancelled, fourteen days confined to barracks! Meanwhile our arduous training continued. For example, we did a 25 kilometre march with full equipment and radio set, which was no easy task. I ended up with the most enormous blisters, which the medical orderlies treated with iodine and powder. (I suspect they hadn't got anything else in the infirmary anyway.) This was followed by night exercises including an orientation race using sketches and prismatic compass. With our unit commander Holzapfel, Schäfer and me we were the winners and were rewarded with time off duty.

In August we went to Wildflecken troop training grounds. The marches, exercises, night alerts, the shooting and radio practices were all even worse than before. Every day we fell into our beds completely exhausted. In action later on, we realised time and again how valuable this training had been for us. Sweat saves blood, that was a truism that was often confirmed later. We didn't know it yet though, so we cursed and swore at everything and everyone, at every stripe and every star. However, this tough training eventually began to produce results. After a major Regimental exercise the Signal Communication Platoon was singled out for special praise by Oberstleutnant Grazy, an excellent Austrian officer. After our period at the troop training grounds ended, I never forgot one of our mottos about the damn place: *Lieber den ganzen Arsch voller Zwecken, als vierzehn Tage Wildflecken.* (Better an arseful of nails than two weeks at Wildflecken.)

At around this time our Signal Communication leader Oberleutnant Schuller hatched the brilliant idea of getting us invited to visit the Telefunken radio works in Berlin, a most welcome diversion. When we arrived we were warmly welcomed and given a tour of the works. We were particularly interested in the manufacture of our pack radio sets and their internal workings, since we had already used them in our training. A tasty meal in the works canteen was followed by permission for us to go into Berlin in small groups, sightseeing. The Ku-Damm, Berlin's famous shopping centre, the Kaiser Wilhelm Memorial Church, the radio tower and the first underground train we'd seen. There wasn't anything like that in my small but convivial city of Munich. A wonderful city. Our return to barracks was less entertaining, as the bus broke down and left us stranded and shivering in the cold.

Just about then I developed a plan to make our off duty hours less monotonous and, along with six others, I signed on in the town's only dancing school. The fact that ordinary soldiers like us – even when wearing smart dress uniform – were mixing with the daughters of the 'better' classes in the town, that caused something of a sensation and amused us enormously. At the leaving ball all the participants wore while silk rosettes with ribbons on which the initials of one's current partner were to be stuck. So when Jupp Boms danced with Ilse Buschke, J.B. with I.B. – I don't know, but the whole thing made us laugh out loud.

To Poland

It happened very quickly. On 1st September the alarm came: pack rucksacks, arm weapon containers, deal with your private affairs, be ready. We woke at five, and by seven o'clock the Regimental staff and Regimental Signal Communication Platoon were on the move towards Silesia. We were heading for Liegnitz, presumably to our operations airfield. We arrived at 12.30 hours and moved into regular barracks – then we listened to the Führer's grandiose speech, and heard the declaration of war. (Perhaps many of us listened with a degree of scepticism, but I can no longer remember. I only know that it was our dearest wish to make a drop and get into action.) After being woken at 07.00 hours, we were also told about the incredibly rapid advance of our army units and the daring feats of the Luftwaffe. Although genuinely enthusiastic, we were also secretly afraid that the whole war might be over before we could get into action. That would be unbearable.

Initially I got put on telephone duty, which I was due to start at 18.45 hours. Unfortunately, I only emerged from the canteen at 19.15 hours, having had a few to drink. Of course, I was put on another charge. It suddenly occurred to me that, damn it, the infringement might keep me here and stop me getting into action. But among all the preparations 'they' forgot about me. A real slice of luck!

When we heard that Britain had declared war we were delighted. Young and hotheaded as we were, we couldn't imagine anything better than the chance to get our revenge on England. You must remember that a vivid image of Germany's enemies had been drummed into us in the various sections of the Hitler Youth, and in the Labour Service as well.

Though it was a beautiful city, Liegnitz no longer had any attraction for us. The more we heard about the advances by our soldiers, the more restless we got, until finally we were told that we'd be making a drop next morning. We all beamed and hugged each other, totally confident that we'd be successful and wipe the smiles off Polish faces. But when morning came we learned that the operation had been postponed because our armoured units, our Panzers, were already breaking through to Warsaw and we weren't needed. It was enough to drive you crazy. Disarm the aircraft again, re-load the receivers for the wireless transmitters and so on. At least we had time to acquaint ourselves with the anti-aircraft machine gun. After this disappointment we were allowed to go out and console ourselves with the girls, and we damn well needed it.

After a few days there was another big Führer speech, and then a sudden alert at 23.00 hours. Everything was packed again and the barracks and sick-bays cleaned. This time we actually left by lorry at 05.00 hours, not to the airfield but by motorway to Breslau on the border. After passing a few anti-tank obstacles, we reached the first Polish villlages with their characteristic thatched roofs. The roads were miserable, no asphalt or flagstones, and the people on the roadsides looked filthy and ragged. We passed through villages which had been completely destroyed, burned down and shot to pieces during our advance. There were a lot of Jews, in caftans and wearing full beards, among the ruins. Soon we had 25cm of sand under our wheels and couldn't see anything for dust. Night fell, and at 24.00 hours we reached Za Jezierze near Deblin, stopping for the night at a railway station. For the time being we were to remain here, so as a consolation they let us take a look at the Deblin airfield. Everything had been wrecked by bombs, there were large numbers of Polish aircraft lying on the ground, burned out. However, there was still a lot of clothes and small pieces of equipment around, which was collected and taken back over the border by Wehrmacht units and Labour Service detachments on the principle of 'finder's keepers'. In any case, the rumour was spreading that the Vistula was going to be the new border between Russia and Germany, so that everything that hadn't been nailed down was being taken away. I managed to obtain good milk from a local farmer in exchange for a couple of cigarettes, and used the opportunity to learn my first Polish words, like Jaiko, Meleko, Cleb, Fara. We were housed in a modern barracks. It wasn't completely finished, but it was actually something of a miracle that the place was still standing at all. The old, small barrack buildings must have been dreadful, so far as you could tell – even our barracks in Stendal were palaces by comparison. Here too there was equipment everywhere, and we organised little souvenirs for ourselves – I got a gas mask and a bayonet. To stop us getting too depressed there were constant inspections of weapons, equipment, uniform. I actually managed to avoid being caught out during these, which was really saying something. Along the bend of the Vistula there were great casemates full of bars of copper, lead, zinc in enormous quantities. Everything, absolutely everything, was loaded up and brought back to the Reich. Next day we were moved out at 04.00 hours, by lorry. Wherever we were heading, it was all the same to us. There was a certain amount of sporadic shooting going on, but nothing that would require our attention. We were the ace of trumps of the German Wehrmacht, but we hadn't been allowed to prove ourselves in battle. We travelled through Random-Kielce to Wies Ztyno, about forty kilometres from Czechenstochau, often seeing Jews from the East in their characteristic clothing being made to do clearing work. We established our quarters in the schoolhouse of a village which had remained almost undamaged, but had hardly unpacked our gear when we were ordered out again. The staff officers had noticed our decent accommodation and wanted it for themselves. It's the same the whole world over – the ones on the top have the whip hand over the poor sods at the bottom.

I was told to report to the Company Commander yet again, expecting another rocket up the backside – only to hear, as I snapped to attention – that I was being promoted to Gefreite. Frankly, I didn't care a rap for the promotion itself, but it meant a bit more pay, and maybe it would be my turn to bully the new ones in the garrison for a change. I was assigned to Dabrovan to 1 Anti-Tank Defence Company, radio contact to the Regiment. Such rubbish, the war was over now, without us. We weren't even happy at home, when we returned there the day after. We stopped in Magdeburg, and then the population of Stendal turned out to welcome us as heroes with apples, cigarettes and flowers. The truth was, we never got the chance to be heroes in Poland. Back to barracks, and to room 9. In the evenings, back into the town where Elfi, Ruth, Inge, Ilse, Dagmar and the others were waiting for us. And to Coffee House Niedlich, the Vaterland tavern, the Tavern am See. Of course I got back late again, not in time for lights-out, and got into more trouble. Two days later Oberjäger Schönfeld caught me as I sneaked back late yet again and this time I got two days' close arrest for which I reported on Monday, 23 October 1939, armed with notebooks, books and cigarettes. No cells were available – none ever were – so they divided a room by putting wardrobes across the length of it and sticking strips of paper above. But they overlooked this detail by the window so I was able to slip through, sleep on straw mattresses in the other part of the room and visit my comrades through the window there – really rather neat, don't you think? Christ, a couple of Oberjäger almost caught me when I threw a dog-end out of the window, but they couldn't prove it was me. In the middle of November Schönfeld reported me for 'Mockery of the NCOs meeting'. That boozer! My reward was extra drill and confinement to barracks. Why can't I keep my trap shut? Yet again I had to report in full war paint to the Commander, Oberleutnant Schuller. He was a Tyrolean, rather older than the rest and with a slight limp, but a great bloke. 'Pöppel,' he said, 'if you carry on like this then you'll end up in the punishment battalion.' There was nothing I could do except perform a smart about-face.

Training continued – there were jumping exercises, radio exercises for the Regiment and the Division. Usually we called at farmhouses during these, and I'll never forget the fantastic farmers' breakfasts served up by their friendly and obliging wives. Some quiet months followed, with the evenings set aside for the girls. Despite our paratroopers' bonus, our pay was no longer enough to keep us entertained. Once I even had to flog my ring to the waiter from the Tavern am See. But that's why we've got mothers, mine always helped out.

Wonders will never cease! Out of the clear sky came four days of home leave, God knows why. Not a moment too soon, since I only had enough money for the train fare home and couldn't even afford a beer on the platform. But there was great rejoicing at home when I arrived. I wasn't allowed to take off the smart dress uniform with its shiny belt and green stripes on with the arm with the inscription *1 Fallschirmjägerregiment*. Relatives, acquaintances, school-friends all wanted to see me and in the evenings, of course, I was bathed and anointed for the trip into Munich for the dancing. And the girls! One particularly attractive one with brown doe eyes really took my fancy. She was sitting with an Unteroffizier from an anti-aircraft artillery unit, but once she'd had a dance with me he was fuming with rage. He had no chance against a Gefreite from the Parachute Regiment.

I'd hardly arrived back in Stendal when I got a rocket from Feldwebel Moser because my cap was askew. If I'd only got it on properly then I wouldn't have been out in the cold for leave at Christmas and New Year. Some people had to stay behind, so naturally I was one of them. My ma sent a giant food parcel, which at least made the days easier to bear.

In the middle of January we had a pleasant surprise. It was 'Strength Through Joy' for soldiers (translator's note: *Kraft durch Freude*, or Strength Through Joy, was the name of the Nazi leisure organisation), which meant we had been invited on a ski course in the Harz mountains, at Braunlage. I told my parents to send my best hickory skis on to me by train. Braunlage proved to be a pretty little town with wonderful coffee houses where we could dance with local girls and excellent ski slopes, long downhill runs through the woods. My comrades were happy to fool about, but of course I went at breakneck speed, eager to show off and be the undisputed champion skier. It didn't last. I was determined to make one really fast run, but failed to spot some bumps in the ground. Though I managed to take the first lot, the next ones catapulted me into the air, where I performed two dramatic somersaults and broke my beautiful skis at the front and back. Pride goes before a fall, as the saying goes.

Phips Dietrich and I went walking and got to know two sweet girls. We went dancing with them a couple of times, but nothing else happened. First they were too young and second they were too well brought up for us to get round them so quickly. I can only assume that this resistance fascinated me so much that it explains why – when I returned from prisoner-of-war camp later – I married one of these girls, Gerda.

Meanwhile, our military training was getting even tougher. Full alerts, night marches at brisk pace, radio drills. Everything was pointing to an operation in the near future. In May 1940 the Regimental staff was transferred to Paderborn in strict secrecy, with confinement to barracks, no post. After a few false alarms, this was it at last.

The drop over Holland

German paratroopers dropping over Holland, in a photograph taken by a Dutch amateur photographer.

In the Regimental Signal Communications Platoon leader's aircraft during the flight to Holland. On the left, Oberleutnant Schuller, behind on the left Jäger Becker and Jäger Güttler.

In Dordrecht, street barricades were erected against the paratroopers.

Paratroopers guard the approach roads.

The first houses of Dordrecht in flames.

The ruined goods station.

Supplies being dropped for the paratroopers.

Heavy mortar in action.

Paratroop dispatch rider on the motorway in Holland.

On 13 May 1940 the first German armoured scout cars passed through the paratroopers' positions on the road to Rotterdam. German tank troops link up with the paratroopers who had landed earlier. Hauptmann Gericke (right) in conversation with men from the 9th Armoured (Panzer) Division.

The first armoured scout cars reach the paratroopers' positions. On the left, (opposite page) Regimental Commander Oberst Bruno Bräuer and Oberleutnant Count von der Schulenburg.

German surgical hospital in Dordrecht.

Dutchmen recover their wounded.

Dordrecht capitulates. The
white flag is raised over the
Cathedral on 14 May.

Parachute drop in Holland
10 May 1940

A beautiful, cloudless day. Early in the morning the heavy-laden aircraft take off, gain height and fly across the border into Holland. There are aircraft filling the sky like flocks of birds gathering in the autumn. Stukas and fighters above and below us, a powerful armada. After a scattering of anti-aircraft fire the signal came through: 'Prepare to jump!' It's 05.10 hours. We jump and float to earth without coming under fire, down to a flat countryside, criss-crossed by ditches. A tug on the cords, another to get me over a ditch since I have no desire to get wet. Roll forwards like we were taught, run under the parachute, unfasten it and race to the containers of weapons and radio equipment. We quickly establish contact with HQ and the men assemble. Then we have time to rest in a pretty little house, with tea still warm on the table and the bread already buttered. At first we don't see any people at all, they'll all be hiding from the Huns, of course. Then we hear a field telephone report that Dutch soldiers from a barracks or a farm 500 metres away are shelling the roads and have already knocked out one of our field telephones. Immediately, Oberleutnant Schuller calls for volunteers and Güttler, Fleischman, Sepp Geyersberger, Hans Becker, Jupp Boms, Sascha Surowka and I take off with the Commander. We crawl to the hedges and Hans Fleischmann, a fine, quiet fellow, goes down. He ventured out too far and has been shot and killed instantaneously. The Commander calls for heavy machine guns and we stay under cover for a while. But then he just can't wait any longer. He shouts 'Attack, go go' and we leap out into the open. Suddenly we're caught by gunfire from the roofs. Geyersberger is hit and Oberleutnant Schuller goes down with a serious bullet wound in the belly. Boms drags him back under cover, but he says he's done for and tells us to look after Geyersberger. Typical of him – a marvellous officer, always putting other people first. But Geyersberger is already dying, there is nothing we can do for him.

On the left by the farmstead there is a small outbuilding and I set off for it with desperate strides. When I reach a window, it's to discover a little soldiers' canteen, empty. Fighting to get my breath, I even have time to drink some chocolate as I look cautiously out to get my bearings. The farmstead is ony eight metres away and there are just a few Dutchmen on guard at the windows, but all of them are shooting wildly and at random towards the front. At last I hear the sound of our machine-guns, making the enemy take cover and giving me the chance to jump out, my 08 pistol in the left hand and a grenade in the right. I reach the makeshift barracks and duck down under the window. In goes the grenade, on to the next window. As they hear screams from inside and the whinnying of horses, my comrades charge forwards, seizing their chance. More hand grenades go in before a white cloth is chucked out and the garrison surrenders. Sixty-three Dutchmen come out – and there were only twelve of us. (As it turned out I was awarded the Iron Cross First Class for this episode, although I didn't find out about it till later.) Another room-mate Dinkel from Bamberg, was killed during the last assault on the barracks; we find his body lying twisted on the ground. We have seen our first men killed . . . and stand before them in silence.

Oberleutnant Schuller was taken to a hospital in Dordrecht, but died of his wounds the next day. Today our comrades lie together in the Dutch cemetary at Ysselsteyn near the German border: Oberleutnant Schuller, Karl Dinkel, Hans Fleischmann and Sapp Geyersberger. Jupp Boms often visits them there and takes flowers in tribute to the comrades-in-arms of our youth.

We take our prisoners to the regimental command post and get our new orders there. It's a tiny place, with only a couple of houses and a street. Wild rumours are beginning to circulate among the men, like 'the English are coming with motor torpedo-boats', 'they're landing', or 'we're surrounded'. The Commander, Oberstleutnant Bräuer, stands above us on the wall, wearing only a cap instead of his steel helmet, and surveys the surrounding area through his telescope. Shells come crashing down and an officer yells 'Take cover, Oberstleutnant!' Bräuer answers with his unmistakable stammer: 'Paratroopers never come under fire!' But as the bombardment grows heavier even he is forced to get under cover. Wounded men are brought in and given makeshift treatment, a process which continues until nightfall. We sleep among them, wherever we can find room. The place reeks of sweat and blood, comrades are groaning and crying out, rasping terribly, one of them draws his last breath almost beside me. It will be a very long time before I can forget the appalling, inhuman sound. So this is war, this is the action that we have been longing for so much. Later on we heard a lot of drivel about the heroic remarks dying soldiers were said to have made. You know, all that stuff about 'Farewell, my Führer, farewell, my Fatherland, give my love to my parents, my God have mercy on me'. I never heard anything like that. I only saw them die.

Next morning a Dutch bicycle company attacks in almost copybook style. They put their cycles together about three hundred metres away from us, line up, attack us on a wide front – an officer with a pistol at their head. We have to let them get close before opening fire, since there are so few of us against them.

We spend the day sending raiding parties to Dordrecht and on reconnaissance. Our situation is far from rosy, but the Commander's calmness is very infectious and there's great jubilation in the morning when our own tanks break through to us from the south. We've held on, and we've done it. In the next few days the first Iron Crosses Second Class are awarded for our part in the defeat of Holland, and I'm among them. (Of course I was terrifically proud, being just nineteen years old at the time.) Shortly afterwards we are sent back to our garrison town, although the Blitzkrieg is continuing elsewhere. We have come through our great baptism of fire. Wherever we go in Germany the paratroopers are celebrated, and the world is forced to take note of the powerful new weapon at the heart of the Wehrmacht. There are no longer any islands – and England is near. Now a parachute drop on England would really be something, damn it, and we'd surely be the spearhead for any attack. For the moment, though, the Army needs us elsewhere.

Narvik 1940

The situation in Narvik is becoming critical for our sailors and mountain infantry, who are surrounded there. The 1st Battalion of the Parachute Regiment under Major Walter is being sent to reinforce them, so they can hold out until the main force of our mountain infantry reaches Narvik after an arduous cross-country march. We are taken to Drontheim by lorry, ship and train, to an airfield which is still usable, and exchange our jumping boots for heavily nailed climbing boots. I'm not bothered by this at all, being well used to wearing them in the hills at home, but to my comrades from north Germany they feel like lead. We are also provided with wonderful oiled Norwegian pullovers, knee-protectors and other equipment. After a few days we set out for the far north. So far as I recall, we're flying with extra fuel tanks and two men fewer. Nevertheless, it's still very cramped in the aircraft, and extemely cold. Occasionally we are overtaken by fighters protecting our plane. Then the call comes: 'Prepare to jump'.

The aircraft descends to 80 metres and we jump close to Björnfeld on the Swedish border. Crucifix, then I plunge into the snow by an enormous boulder. The drop has gone well again. For accommodation we find little wooden huts, warm and cosy. It doesn't get dark at night here, only dusk – the midnight sun is a new experience for me. Next day we move forward to reinforce the line, which is slowly but inexorably being forced to retreat in a semicircle towards the border. In fact, we're already discussing the prospect of internment in Sweden and being inspected by the Swedish border soldiers when we suddenly get the message 'Tommy has gone'. Silently, secretly, and to us quite inexplicably, the British had slipped away. Later in the war, we were to be confronted by this ability of the Tommies to mount a skilful retreat on a number of occasions.

We pack our stuff together in record time and travel by trolley and on foot down the mining railway to Narvik. To left and right of the tracks there are enormous quantities of abandoned equipment. In

Reinforcements for Narvik.

Above Norway's fiords.

Paratroopers landed by the airfield of Stavanger Stola.

Gefreite Martin Pöppel at Drontheim airfield before the flight to Narvik.

From 26 May to 1 June 1940 the units of I Battalion were dropped near Björnfell station by the Swedish border, from Ju 52/3m aircraft.

The drop begins.

Two paratroopers are blown off course, the rest gather.
Narvik falls on 9 June 1940.

In single file to the positions.

The English withdrew under cover of darkness, taking us completely by surprise. I Battalion loads its heavy equipment onto trolleys and marches down to Narvik along the mining railway around which there had been heavy fighting (left). Above: assembling in Narvik harbour, with Gefreite Schäfer second from the right.

When the German paratroopers reach the port of Narvik on 9 June 1940, the battle has already been fought. The British have withdrawn secretly.

The Battalion in Narvik before embarkation on the cruiser Nuremburg.

Rombakken fiord we see our warships, half-submerged in the water and destroyed by gunfire – but also plenty of British ships, hit by our Stukas. The harbour and the surrounding houses have been destroyed, otherwise things are not too bad here. The people come out slowly, calm, but looking at us with stony faces. Like ourselves, they can't understand why their friends have bolted. After a couple of days of quiet, we board the cruiser Nuremberg and admire the wonderful snow-topped mountain, the 'Queen', which seems to look down on us all. (I don't know if it was really called the 'Queen', but it was one, to me.) Then a beautiful journey through the fiords, except for the fact that we're completely alone. On more than one occasion we're forced to take cover below decks after an air-raid warning, whilst the Nuremberg slips along the rock face for extra protection. Thank heavens I never joined the navy – I find I absolutely loathe being below decks in an iron coffin, waiting for something to hit. I much prefer to be in the thick of things and see the enemy face to face. Of course, the sailors are very defensive about our funk.

We disembark in Oslo and march through the city. The population has surrendered but they look at us with grim faces. We can't blame them, since we invaded without warning. Then it's home by the freighter – '*Isar*', which makes me nostalgic for Munich: first to the garrison, where we're all awarded the Narvik Shield, and then on home leave.

At this stage I discover that I have been awarded the Iron Cross First Class for Holland, and have been promoted to Oberjäger for courage. But I'd spent all that time since then as a Gefreite, standing to attention in front of the Oberjäger and more or less being forced to polish their boots. I'd been one of them all along and didn't know it – what a joke.

Hardly back from leave when I was assigned to Gardelegen to a newly established Machine-Gun Battalion. As a newly-appointed Oberjäger, decorated with the Iron Cross First and Second Class. I was already a 'somebody': also I was the only Unteroffizier with these decorations in the entire battalion.

Among the officers themselves, only Oberleutnant Otto Laun had the Iron Cross. I came under his command in 2 Company and became a machine-gunner – not a wireless operator any more. The blokes really made me welcome and Feldwebels Eugen Scherer and Willi Lojewski later became my closest friends. Lojeswki was a real mercenary. In his youth he had been with the East Prussian Border Guard, then in the Reichswehr, had volunteered for service in Spain, and was now with us. He was proud to be the only man among us to wear the Spain Cross, and whenever he pushed his cap back in a tavern and shouted: 'This round's on me!', then we knew to watch out. He knocked back Schnapps like the rest of us drank water.

Ours was a fine company. The Commander was incredibly active and resourceful, he lived for his outfit. During this period I learned about the machine gun, about aiming circles and the use of heavy mortars. To this day I don't understand a word of it, though needless to say I was a good shot! Our best machine-gunners were Rudi Frisch and Otto Pfemfert, who had both had training in peacetime.

Rudi Schmidt and Heinz Mülders were our *Hauptgefreite* and they were reliable marksmen as well. Ludwig Pernpeintner was a real specimen, a brawny and rebellious oaf from Lower Bavaria. But you couldn't get anything on him, since he already had the highest grade for non-officers as a Staff Lance Corporal or *Stabsgefreite*. He certainly gave Hauptfeldwebel Wild a whole stack of problems. Yes, these *Hauptgefreite* and *Stabsgefreite* could really give their superiors a rough time. Moreover, they were always careful to commit some major or minor misdemeanour so they wouldn't get promoted. They were brave fellows but they just wanted to go their own way and stay the pride of the troop. As the war years passed this didn't help them because experienced soldiers like them became indispensable. Rudi Schmidt, for one, was made a Feldwebel despite all his efforts to avoid it. Of the rest, I recall lively little August Kruscek, the man we called 'the Russian', because he spoke fluent Polish and had good basic knowledge of Russian as well.

The little town was pretty and the girls no less so. I soon felt really at home at Mutti Knetsch's, the German House and the other joints. After a training course in which I came out top I was promoted early to Feldwebel and accepted into that special circle of men. They were great fellows. Once, when we smashed up the German House after the landlord refused to serve us, all the men put up an iron front, each refusing to give the others away.

In March 1941 we went to the troop training camp at Grafenwöhr for two weeks shooting practice. Then from 19th-23rd March we had a really murderous march exercise to Bayreuth, Waismain and Kueps near Kronach. When I took off my boots in Bayreuth the pus and filth was running down my legs, blisters on top of other blisters, but I put iodine on and went to the dance anyway (though I have to admit that I trod very gingerly). These weeks were exhausting, but they hardened us and made us desperate for our next action. We reckoned one was imminent – it was only a question of when and where.

In April Oberleutnant Büttner came from 3 Company to our 2 Company. Like Feldwebels Calame and Strohschein, he was on a form of probation from the special elite Nazi schools, the *Ordensschulen*. We found them good blokes, especially our new Commander after he staged a good comrades' evening for us, full of entertainment and laughter. From the officers down to the last driver, we had become a family. We were ready.

Crete, Our Island of Destiny

On 2 May we entrain at the little station of Solpke near Gardelegen. The journey takes us through Berlin, Dresden, Teschen-Bodenbasch, Prague, Gmund, Vienna, Heygeschalen and Gyoer to Budapest. There on the station we have a few hours of rest, so our band plays for us with Oberleutnant Büttner on the accordion and Pfemfert on the drums. A gipsy boy comes near and plays us some lovely Hungarian tunes on his fiddle, and we give him some of our cigarettes to show our appreciation. Then on through Szeged and Mako to Arad on the Hungarian-Rumanian border, where we disembark on 6 May.

Next we find ourselves travelling by lorry through Timisoara, Lugoj and Caransebes to Orsova on the Danube facing the Iron Gate (I remember from my schooldays, not so long ago after all, that Emperor Trajan once passed through there). On 7 May we're off again through Turnu-Severin and Craiova to Caracal. On 8 May we cross the Danube at Turnu-Magurela, over a bridge built by the army engineers, and find ourselves in Bulgaria. The journey continues through Pleven, Lovec, Watesgrad, Botevgrad and Sofia to Dupnica, which we reach on 9 May.

It's hard work for our drivers on these dusty roads. I usually travel as the passenger in a motorcycle side-car, and whenever I doze off my helmet knocks against the handlebars. When we take off our goggles we look like antediluvian monsters in our heavy cycling gear and with great white patches on faces which are otherwise caked with dust. There's a gipsy camp not far from the road, so when we stop they come over to us to beg, and the ugly older woman bare their breasts. The only things of interest to us are their heavy gold bangles, ear rings and necklaces, but we have to be careful, as they try to steal everything that isn't nailed down. An undefinable, rather sweet smell hangs around them, and we're happy to move off again.

On 10 May we reach the heavily defended Metaxa line north of Salonika, then the town itself and Elasson, where we can admire Mount Olympus, still covered with snow.

Through the Balkans

At the central station in Budapest. At the beginning of March 1941 the Battalion sets off by train for an unknown destination. To assist the disguise, all references to 'paratroopers' are removed, including the jumpers badge. The Machine Gun Battalion's band plays to keep spirits up before the departure. Left to right: Fahnenjunker-Feldwebel Calame, Gefreit Buderus, Oberfeldwebel Strohschein, Gefreite Herzog, Company Commander Oberleutnant Büttner (with accordion), Oberfeldwebel Hütterer, Gefreite Kienast, Gefreite Pfemfert and Oberjäger Zeller. Already in the train: Feldwebel Eugen Scherer.

Our railway journey ended in Rumania and we continued by lorry and motorcycle.

Gypsies begged from us on our way through the Balkans.

On 8 May 1941 the Battalion crossed the Danube at Turnu-Magurela over a temporary bridge built by Army engineers, and continued through Bulgaria to Greece.

To Crete

To Crete. On 15 May 1941 the Battalion reaches Tanagro and camps in olive groves near this Greek advanced airfield. On 19 May the operation order for Crete arrives: on 20 May, Rethymnon airfield in the centre of the island is to be captured. In front of the aircraft before setting off at 13.00 hours. Left to right: Hauptmann Mölders, Oberfeldwebel Hütterer, Feldwebel Dominiak, Hauptfeldwebel Wild, Oberjäger E. A. Müller and Obergefreite Rohrmann.

Oberfeldwebel Hütterer and Feldwebel Dominiak (both killed on 20 May 1941) climb in to the Ju 52.

Oberleutnant Dr Büttner Company Commander (killed on 21 May 1941).

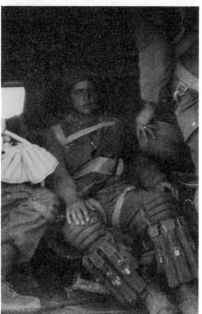

To Crete, wearing the same battledress as in Norway – but now with the temperature at 45 degrees in the shade.

On 12 May we travel through more mountain passes to Larissa, and then to the legendary pass at Thermopylae. It's narrow, lots of ravines, with vehicles here and there which have been shot up and destroyed. There are soldiers everywhere, patching things together again and getting them started, but this is an arduous climb for our excellent drivers. On the 13th we encamp at Levadia and have time to wash and stretch our tired limbs. Yet despite the hardships, for our drivers especially, it has been a fascinating journey so far. The beautiful countryside of the Danube with the Iron Gate, Olympus and the harbour at Salonika, they've offered some compensation for our discomforts. Then we've observed with interest the multiplicity of different peoples along the way: we aren't impressed with the Rumanians, think them lazy and dirty at first (an impression later confirmed); then the cleaner and more cheerful Saxons; the nomadic gipsies with their tents blackened by soot and smoke; then the big men of Bulgaria, who have rightly been described as the Prussians of the Balkans – clean, well dressed, and well-disposed towards us.

The attitude of the Bulgarians is obviously based on the comradeship in arms of the First World War. They offer us strawberries and honey, which is still expensive and it's so early in the season. Out of friendship, and not for money or payment in kind.

Less impressive – at least till now – the Greeks. We'd all learned about the blonde Hellenes in our childhood (I'm thinking of Otto in my home town of Ottobrunn, who said farewell to his father and left to be King of Greece. And of Klenze, who built the new Athens). But the people we see look completely different – small, black-haired, more concerned to haggle and to bargain than to work. Only the little shoe-shine boys are lively, offering us their 'extra top class Stuka shine' to make us laugh. They have been quick to learn a little German, and 'Stuka' is their word for everything that is best and most beautiful. After this much-needed rest we reach Tanagro on the 15th, making camp under the olive trees in captured English tents. In the Hitler Youth movement we had all learned to be smart and neat, so there's great activity as we clean and polish our weapons and equipment. Lojewski has sunburn on his left shoulder and is getting it treated, others are shaving off the beards they have acquired, and we're playing skat. And there is great jubilation when we discover that our crafty drivers, going to get supplies in Athens, have managed to get hold of German beer. Our Hauptfeldwebel Gerhard Wild, who is known as 'Cap'n Wild' and is almost like a mother to us, sends a lorry to fetch some of these crates of beer and we keep it cold by storing it in a hole in the ground.

On 19 May we received our orders for the next day – a parachute drop on the island of Crete. (We reckoned that such a small island wouldn't be a problem for us. How wrong we were – it was to be an enormous and bloody task). That evening we gathered under a huge olive tree, drank beer and sang our songs accompanied by Oberleutnant Büttner's band. Was it premonition that we didn't just sing cheerful soldiers' songs as usual, but also included nostalgic songs of home? For most of the men it would be the first parachute jump and only a few – such as myself – knew what death in action was really like. Maybe many realised, even had a premonition, that they might be killed. No one commented on it. But many of these lads, so fresh and young and so full of optimism, were to fall in battle during the next few days.

The night passes quickly because all of us are thinking of home, of parents, friends and fiancées. Even the toughest soldiers can dream.

In the early morning of 20 May the sky is full of the drone of aircraft setting off for the dropping zones. We reach ours at midday. (The plan was for us to take the airfield at Rethymnon in the centre of the island, on the assumption that the enemy would concentrate on the dropping zones at Cania and Heraklion. But this didn't happen. The enemy already had the information it needed, obtained by radio contact with the mainland.)

The last preparations are made, the battle orders distributed to the platoons, the aerial photographs studied carefully. The airfield and the area round Rethymnon are to be taken by 2 Parachute Regiment with two Battalions and 13 and 14 Companies under the command of Oberst Sturm. 2 Parachute Artillery Battalion under Oberleutnant Thorbecke, 1 Company Parachute Anti-Aircraft and the Parachute Machine Gun Battalion without 3 Company are also assigned to the Regiment. Later, we learned that the enemy forces in the battle sector were 19th Australian Brigade under General Vasey, six Greek battalions and anti-aircraft, artillery and light armoured units.

The men board the lorries, whilst I travel as passenger with Misloviky and the sidecar to the airfield nearby. It's dusty again, and gets even more so when the first aircraft return from the dropping zones, some with large bullet holes in their wings and fuselage. Over to the planes, ready with the aerial-delivery containers and then – if you didn't laugh you'd cry – we have to fill up the Junkers petrol tanks by hand! Finally, wearing our heavy packs, we go to the machines. A last wave, and climb in, setting off at 13.00 hours. At first we stay at high altitude and fly over the first Greek islands in blazing sunshine, but when we reach the open sea we start flying low. Flying time will be over two hours, so I use the opportunity to grab some sleep. It's a blessed ability, one that I can use at any time of day or night.

When we see a mountain range in the distance, we know that we are near Crete. We check our gear one more time, particularly the fastener on the end of the jump line. The aircraft achieves the correct height for the drop and soon we're over the coast. 'Prepare to jump' – signal – and out. My God, we've been lucky. Our jumpmaster has located the dropping zone perfectly and at 15.40 hours we drift to earth, about 12km east of the town of Rethymnon and 1.5km north of Episkopi. Miki and I end up in an olive tree, but one somersault and we're on the ground. During the drop there's been nothing more threatening than a few shots. After a short time the Company has assembled, and it appears that just one aircraft complement has been put down in the wrong place and is missing. Even now, as we fetch the weapons containers, we're getting damnably hot – the heat is almost 50 degrees and we're all breathing heavily already. First of all we just have to get acclimatised to it. Clearly our leaders were well aware of the heat, but we've been sent into battle in full uniform and with para jumping overalls as well. Absolutely bloody crazy! We're scarcely likely to be pleased with our rations of salty ham either. It's not long before some men, myself included, have taken off their jackets and hidden them in the undergrowth.

We advance on both sides of the coast road, following our objectives of occupying the airfield with units of 2 Regiment and Major Kroh. But we don't get very far. In the hills round the airfield we come under heavy fire and are forced to leave the road and move south through the vineyards in order to make our attack. By the time we reach the first hill, twilight is falling. The place has already been evacuated by elite troops from New Zealand. We were later to discover that the New Zealanders were regarded as the best troops in the Empire, but they soon sensed the kind of German troops they were up against here. We move down again to the coast road. In Episkopi the entire battle group is gathering for the attack on the airfield. As a precaution, a few road blocks are quickly set up, and then we get our orders. Our platoon under Leutnant Rikowski, with the first group under Oberfeldwebel Scherer and the second under me, is ordered to penetrate the vineyards on the left of the coast road. We advance stealthily in the darkness, whispering the password

'Reich Marshal' whenever we run into other troops we can't recognise. Now we know which direction the enemy is, but not exactly where.

In the grey light of morning we storm the vineyards on the hills at the edge of the airfield. Now our objective is before us. But they've spotted us and give us hell – and real hell at that. I see one badly injured Oberjäger holding his torn abdominal wall closed with both hands. When we stop to help him he just says: 'Get down there first, then fetch me!' Unbelievable. Oberjäger Rudi Freisch has the most enormous stroke of luck. He gets a bullet through the nose, but it goes in one side and clean out the other. (After a few days he could even blow his nose again.)

It's no good. People are getting hit all around us, and the air is full of their groans and cries of pain. We're forced to withdraw from this hill of blood and so fail to achieve our objective. Firing continues on both sides. We manage to find some cover on the rear slope, then move quickly to a white house where we can care for our wounded. The medical orderlies really have their hands full now. Then to a shallow ditch, and leap over the road into a little hollow. How many of us are there now, thirty men, forty? A heated debate follows. An Oberleutnant Hintz or Hintze from another unit wants to give the order to surrender. A Feldwebel replies curtly: 'Quite out of the question'.

Soon we hear the noise of vehicles, and orders being given in English. The only road still free is the one leading to the coast, so we move down through the bushes and the undergrowth. Everything that isn't absolutely indispensable – except weapons and ammunition – is jettisoned to make the going easier. We move along by the coast for a good hour, sometimes wading along in the sea up to our chests when that's the only way forward. Some stragglers from other units have managed to make their way to us, until finally – worn out – we reach another group of soldiers on a small hill. Under the command of Oberleutnant van Roon, a new battle group is being put together there. Oberjäger Frisch hands me my first cigarette – my God, I needed that. Tired and dispirited, we sit there with bowed heads. To top our astonishment, we discover that our East Prussian Leutnant Rikowski has turned on his heels and escaped here without his weapons and hardly any uniform. Well, we can understand most of it, but how the hell did Rikowski (who's normally so reliable) ever leave his gun behind?

A bitter victory

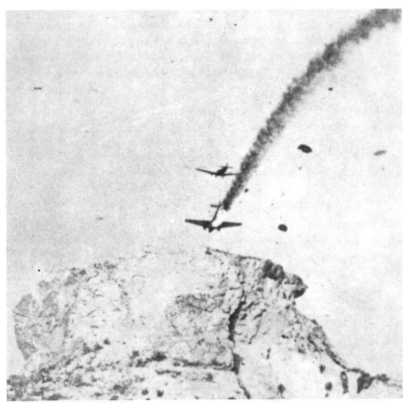

British, Australian and New Zealand forces had been stationed on Crete since 29 October 1940, one day after Mussolini's attack on Greece. In May 1941, when the Greek mainland was already occupied by German troops, the Armed Forces High Command (OKW) decided to make a landing on Crete, on the suggestion of the man who later became Commanding General of XI Airborne Corps, Generalleutnant Kurt Student. It was only 590 km from this Greek island to Alexandria. At the end of some extraordinarily bitter fighting some 6000 Germans, including 3764 airborne troops, had died for their victory.

There are few photographs of the murderous battle for Crete. German war artists used the customary 'heroic style' to give sketchy impressions of the inferno. The reality was generally indescribable.

After the arrival of the mountain infantry, the battle is over. The remainder of 2 Company marches from the last hills to the town of Rethymnon. At the head is Leutnant Rikowsky and, from left: Oberfeldwebel Lojewski and Feldwebel Scherer and Pöppel.

Feldwebel Scherer in the side-car on a tour of inspection.

The vineyard 'Blood Mountain' at Rethymnon.

Es starben den Heldentod auf Kreta unsere geliebten Söhne, Brüder, Enkel und Neffen

der Ritterkreuzträger

Wolfgang Graf von Blücher
Oberleutnant in einem Fallschirmjägerregiment im Alter von 24 Jahren

Leberecht Graf von Blücher
Gefreiter in einem Fallschirmjägerregiment im Alter von 19 Jahren

Hans=Joachim Graf von Blücher
Jäger in einem Fallschirmjägerregiment im Alter von 17 Jahren.

Darze, Post Stuer, in Mecklenburg
Posen und Altengottern, den 23. Juni 1941

Gertrud v. Nordheim, geb. Freiin Marschall, verw. Gräfin Blücher
Ludwig v. Nordheim, Gaulandwirt im Luftgau II
Elisabeth Gräfin v. Blücher
Adolf Graf v. Blücher, Leutnant zur See
Gertrud Gräfin v. Blücher
Richenza v. Nordheim
Wilhelmine Freifrau Marschall, geb. Gräfin Rittberg
Charlotte Freiin Marschall

Three brothers from a famous military family died as paratroopers on Crete. The oldest was 24 and the youngest just 17 years old.

The memorial cemetery of 2 Regiment and the Machine Gun Battalion at Rethymnon, and graves of the fallen.

The Cretans, occupied and oppressed for centuries by foreign peoples, fought against the German invasion with all possible means. Despite some eventual improvement in relations with the occupiers, atrocities continued to take place long after the battle for Crete was over.

Returning home in summer 1941. Gardelegen welcomes 'its' Machine Gun Battalion home with a victory arch. All the men were decorated with the Iron Cross First or Second Class for their part in the conquest of Crete.

New units are assembled from the remaining men and a defensive line is established. Anxious questions among us: 'How will things go?' 'How are the others doing?' 'Can we break through to Heraklion?' Despite our tiredness and despondency, hardly anyone gets any sleep. In the morning I get the order to recce the coast road and find out whether there are enemy troops there. I take six men for the job. On the left is a steep slope, the right side is almost flat but at least it's covered by a good deal of undergrowth and scattered olive trees. We march in formation and tensely on the alert for three hours towards Heraklion though it's still a long way off. No contact with the enemy, so we can turn round and head back. When we've got to within about 500 metres of our own lines, we hear rifle fire and a burst of machine-gun fire. Creeping cautiously forwards, we see that Cretan partisans wearing armbands, widely spread out, are firing on the Roon battle group. We're able to pick them off from behind and, under fire from two directions, they're quickly forced to pull out. But unfortunately there's one more man we haven't seen because he's further back than the others, who manages to shoot and kill one of my men. We have to bury him there and then. (Long after the war I tried to find his grave again, but without success.)

We report back. Other recce patrols are sent out, some through a deep ravine to a town which has apparently been evacuated by the enemy not long before. It's here that Rikowski get his chance. He's allowed to go into the village alone while we cover him, so that he can recover his self-respect. He completes the job successfully – and after that his inglorious flight is forgotten.

An aid station is set up in a little bay under the hills by the coast, ground panels are set out and marked with stones and identification letters. We have no contact whatsoever with other battle groups, and have very little rations and ammunition left. Finally, though, we're spotted by an HE 111, a Heinkel aircraft, which dips its wings in recognition. Less than two hours later supplies are dropped to us, along with the order to join forces with another battle group based in a nearby oil factory: together, we're to capture the hills ahead. This contact with outside has left us feeling physically and mentally refreshed and we achieve our objective with the help of a 2cm antitank gun which takes the 'white house' apart. After that, the enemy disappears into the mountains. Once the battle groups have been reorganised, our next objective is to make another attack on the airfield where we had suffered so many casualties. But as we advance, we suddenly see motor cycles and jeeps moving towards us.

Fantastic! The mountain infantry has arrived! (The Airborne Assault Regiment, now under the command of that incredible old campaigner Oberst Ramcke, had managed to capture Maleme airfield albeit at tremendous cost. As a result, the superb mountain infantry had been able to land, and the two had joined forces to conquer the hills and drive off the enemy.)

Crete was ours. It was a heroic and bitter struggle but never forget what a tremendous toll it took in the lives of our troops. Winston Churchill was to say that, here on Crete, the spearhead of the German army had leapt to its death. He was right. We never recovered from it.

We marched into Rethymnon, the prisoners dragging our weapons containers. All day we were kept busy with the task of burying our dead. Some had been drowned, having been dropped too soon and pulled under by the weight of their equipment. Other planeloads had landed right in the middle of the enemy positions. Our comrades lay there still, their parachutes behind them, mown down in the order they had jumped. It was said that others had been mutilated. Thank God, I never saw any.

We put up crosses with names and dates, but what good are crosses to our comrades? Young lads like ourselves, cheerful and happy in Tanagro such a short time ago. Now they lie here, far from home. Oberleutnant Büttner, Feldwebel Calame, our friend Feldwebel Fritz Dominiak, Leutnant Schwiefert from the mortar section, Oberfeldwebel Hütterer – all of them gone.

Our oldest jumper, Müller (known as 'EAM') returns to us from his captivity by the British. He'd been a prisoner from 21 to 22 May together with a number of other ranks and with Oberleutnant Fischer. Oberarzt Dr Begus had been dropped with 2 Company of the Parachute Engineer Battalion. Put down accurately and well, they advanced determinedly and, like ourselves, suffered heavy casualties. Although shot through his left forefoot, he worked with orderlies from 3 Company of the Machine Gun Battalion to bury the dead and to care for the wounded. Despite his devoted efforts, many men with stomach and chest wounds could not be saved.

Our Sarge 'Cap'n Wild' had stayed close to our Company Commander, Oberleutnant Büttner. They managed to take prisoner the crew of an immobilised tank and because of their customary decent treatment of these men, Wild had been given a bottle of gin (more than acceptable). Later Wild was wounded in the shoulder and forced to go back for treatment. He discovered later that our brave Commander had been killed, alongside Calame, on the road to the vineyards. We found him there and buried him with the others.

The rest of us have survived, and are eager to exchange our old torn clothing for British tropical uniform. Heinz Hüber sews swimming trunks for everybody so that the Cretan population no longer has any need to be excited or amused at the sight of our alabaster-white bodies on the beaches and in the sea. Oberfeldwebel Lojewski has commandeered a Singer sewing machine for the purpose. We set up our quarters in the first floor of a house on the waterside. Good that we had Oberfeldwebel Scherer with us, since he miraculously attracted all the sand fleas away from the rest of us, until they forced him out into the open air. On a trip to a British ration supply depot in the Suda Bay, we saw how our Stukas had destroyed vast numbers of enemy warships. They were still smoking. It was a mystery to us how our own pilots had been able to land their Ju's at all in the face of all the anti-aircraft positions that we saw.

The enemy had many more men on Crete than we did. Their numerical superiority had only been defeated by the unbroken spirit, the unbreakable will of all our men. But this episode was *not* a glorious chapter in the history of our supreme leadership; instead, it was a glorious chapter in the history of each and every fighting man, whether he was a paratrooper, mountain infantryman, flyer or sailor. And each man honestly deserved his Iron Cross First Class. As I already had mine, I received as consolation one of the relatively few Crete Commemorative Badges from General Student. It consisted of our diving eagle with oak leaf wreath and the inscription 'Crete 1941 in recognition of special merit Feldwebel Pöppel', in metal on black velvet.

Our proud paratroop unit never recovered from the enormous losses sustained on Crete. For us, this was the last major airborne operation of the war. With the war long over, many of us still come back to the island – and not just for a holiday. We make our way to the cemetery at Maleme, to Hill 107 where the fighting was so bitter. 4500 paratroopers, mountain infrantrymen, aircrew and marines are lying there. And if you go through the rows of graves, you'll see that they were almost all young men, eighteen, twenty, twenty-two years old. Among them are the three sons of Count Blücher; an old and famous military dynasty came to an end here on Crete.

For General Student, commander of the airborne forces, Crete was 'a bitter memory'. To General Julius Ringel, popular Mountain Infantry General of the 5th Mountain Infantry Division, it was 'an epic song in a minor key'. And the military historian Liddell Hart wrote: 'It was one of the most astonishing and boldest feats of the war.' But what help are such assessments for our brave comrades who rest there, and whose crosses continue to rebuke us, and to warn?

For the survivors, though, the war went on. We returned to Gardelegen by air and train and the whole population of our garrison town turned out to cheer us as we marched past.

– There are no more islands –

Russia 1941/2

We had heard about the invasion of Russia by our troops whilst we were still in Crete. Even then, we had contemplated the incredible vastness of that country with some trepidation. Now we had got the war on two fronts which the Führer had always wanted to avoid. It didn't feel right to us somehow, made us distinctly uneasy.

Before our first experiences in Russia we spent some time at the Grafenwöhr troop training grounds. Because the Battalion had suffered so many casualties in Crete, we were sent replacements, boisterous young fellows, grand lads just like ourselves. Naturally enough, the youngsters were full of admiration for us, for our decorations and armbands bearing the inscriptions '1 Fallschrimjägerregiment', and 'Crete'. To them we were veterans, though we were only 20 or 22 years of age ourselves.

Another tough period of training began, mainly in the countryside. However, I didn't get to stay to the end, because I was suddenly transferred to an officer training course at the officer candidate school in Dresden-Klotsche. It was strange. One minute I was a Gefreite with Oberleutnant Schuller threatening me with the punishment battalion, the next minute I was an officer candidate. The war had changed so many things. On the course I was nothing special at theory, and I almost stabbed myself through the ear during sword practice. But I was a great deal better at tactics and my operational reports were generally regarded as being very valuable. In December 1941, aged just 21, I was promoted to the rank of Leutnant, or Second Lieutenant.

It's 18 December and we're ready for action again at last. Equipment cleaned, everything in good shape. We're prepared, but no-one knows where we'll be going. The first evidence arrives next day, when I'm ordered to travel to Berlin to fetch shoulder straps for tropical uniform. We all reckon that we'll be going to Africa to help Rommel out. Consequently, there's a great deal of enthusiastic hunting for sunglasses etc. We feel as though we're already in Tobruk, Fort Capuzzo or somewhere, a wonderful sensation. Much laughter and singing accompanies our preparations.

20 December 1941

That night, we find out our mistake. The secret order 'South' has been abandoned and replaced by 'North-East'. A strange feeling – but in the end it doesn't really matter: the most important thing is that we'll soon be in action again. All our preparations are overturned, the tropical gear is withdrawn and replaced by winter clothing. And the stuff that we have to take with us, it's crazy! From double knee pads to foot-cloths, from belly warmers to overcoats and fur coats.

Leutnant Tenschert is transferred to our Company from III/1 – an excellent officer, rather older than me. We hear that we'll get under way on the 24 December, on Christmas Eve of all days, and I am appointed loading officer. We load up in the pouring afternoon rain, first into lorries, then in the evening into the train. Fiancées, wives and friends have been waiting patiently for hours at Gardelegen station so they can say goodbye. Parting is hard and many people are in tears. Finally I report that we're ready for departure and we set off. Which sector will we be sent to, and how many of us will never come back? There's no real Christmas spirit, since each of us is too wrapped up in his own thoughts. Only when the bottles of liquor start circulating does the mood change.

I've forgotten to say that with my promotion I'd been transferred to 1 Company. In one way it was a shame, since I had to leave my best comrades behind – Scherer, Lojewski, Miki – as well as the platoon which was battle-hardened. But at least we were still linked through the Battalion. For now, I'm sharing the compartment with Oberleutnant Ruthe and Inspektor Finner.

We travel through Berlin and Posen, then over the Vistula to Warsaw. Just as when we were travelling to Greece, we pass through old capital cities and places with famous names, and cross rivers whose names we learned off by heart as children. But this time we're not in awe: our destination is Russia, our objective is war and victory. In all honesty the time can't pass quickly enough, we're desperate to be involved in the great struggle again after a delay of nine months. There's no country on earth that exerts such a magnetic attraction on me as bolshevist Russia.

From Warsaw we travel on into Russia itself. We can't see many signs of destruction from the train itself. A few wire entanglements, blockades, a few typical observation towers line the border. However, there are massive differences in the system of soil cultivation. In Germany we're accustomed to a kaleidoscope of ploughed fields, pretty villages, houses with red bricks and little gardens. In Poland things were different, and in Russia they are different again. You can't distinguish fields at all, just a monotonous, bleak landscape. No real villages, only little settlements. Houses? No, only shabby huts made of wood, each one like all the rest. The whole thing makes a dreary and wretched impression on us.

We stop for some time near Bialystock and change engines. A second station building – apparently the Russians have set up a major strategic assembly station here. New installations, big switch control rooms. On the left there's an airfield, with hangars like our own which are already being used by our Luftwaffe. Lots of trains are lined up on the adjoining tracks. Most are transport trains taking wood and coal, machine parts and munitions to the front and returning empty.

A transport train carrying wounded men stops nearby. It's a wretched sight which makes it clear to us how bitterly this war is being fought. It consists of ordinary goods wagons with straw in them for the wounded to lie on. Filthy and louse-ridden, with inadequate dressings and hardly any medical orderlies, no heating – that's how the boys are brought home. As soldiers, we understand the situation better when a railway official explains that there are around 3000 wounded men passing through here every day. Our excellent ambulance trains simply can't cope any more. In the ensuing silence, each of us thinks that a decent soldier's death in action would be better than to be brought home in a train like that, like animals to the slaughter.

Now we're kept busy with our efforts to keep up the spirits of our young, inexperienced soldiers. We order hot water from the engine to wash ourselves and are forced to use sign language, since apart from the train driver and stoker there are only Russians here.

The train sets off again, with the engine and the last carriages occupied by guards with submachine guns to prevent a surprise attack by partisans. There isn't much snow on the land, which is now covered with forest. At regular intervals on the tracks there are little huts occupied by German railway soldiers. They are doing their lonely duty there, protecting the railway line against attack. As we pass we are delighted to exchange greetings, and salute these men we regard as brothers. Out here we really feel the force of the destiny which binds us together as Germans. Here a man looks at other Germans and sees his brother, his home. At home things are different

– people walk straight past each other and only take any notice at marches or rallies.

The train rattles on and soon we reach Minsk, which looks relatively undamaged at first sight. But the snow hides a great deal of devastation and most of it will be ruined. As we have a few hours to kill we go to the German soldiers' home, once a Russian hotel. It looks grandiose from the outside, but not from within. Very basic furniture, no decoration at all in the rooms. However, we enjoy the excellent roast goose served up by the Red Cross, by the attractive nurses in their flattering uniform and red Cossack boots. It can't be easy for these young girls, in enemy territory and so far from home. When we resume our journey we notice vast numbers of small Russian engines, usually destroyed, and huge amounts of ruined equipment. Inspektor Finner tinkers about determinedly till he has made a stove on which we can make some superb coffee.

There's a great deal of chatter, and the bottles are circulating. Everyone still has plenty of goods from the army stores, so the time doesn't drag. But we're no longer drinking for its own sake; now, you get as boozed up as possible since the more you drink the better you can sleep. Oberleutnant Ruthe and I often go into the Sergeants' compartment, where money is changing hands during games of '17 and 4' etc. The more rum the men drink, the bigger the bets. It seems to give Ruthe particular pleasure to take money off me, his youngest Leutnant. He succeeds for some time, but when I'm almost broke I hatch a plan with some of my friends. One of them stands behind Ruthe and nods to tell me when to bid. Pretty soon I'm rolling in money and the chief has to concede defeat. (Later, in Smolensk, we let him in on the trick and shared the money out.) Everyone sits around playing cards to pass the time. The Sarge is lying in the luggage rack above us and sleeping, or at least he's trying to. When he grumbles, everyone lights up a pipe or cigarette and we smoke him out of his lofty perch. Then he clambers down quickly and waits patiently till we need a kip as well. Another day in the life of an ordinary soldier. When we stop, Tenschert and I fetch paliasses from the luggage van, shove them between the upholstered seats and sleep easy. Why didn't we think of it before?

The train chugs on through Russia. We cross the Beresina and reach the major railway junction at Orsa, a massive affair. Even in Tsarist Russia, Orsa had been a major station. The station hall itself is one single huge room, filled with incredible noise and bustle. It's full of soldiers coming back from leave, trying to rejoin their units at

Russia 1941/2

Instead of heading for the Caucasus, most of the Paratroop Machine Gun Battalion flew with units of III Assault Regiment (Sturmregiment) to Rzhev as a 'fire brigade' in order to reinforce the 'balcony' held at great cost of German troops.

Oberleutnant and Company Commander Heinz Ruthe.

Battalion command post near Sobakino. From left: Leutnant Rieke, Leutnant Klitzing, Oberleutnant Ruthe. Far right: Feldwebel Hamm.

Machine-gunners prepare for the counterattack.

Advance from Rzhev airfield
towards Sobakino in the
bitter cold.

For weeks the front at Sobakino was held by the paratroopers, who suffered heavy casualties. Recce patrols guarded against surprise attacks by the Russians. During counterattacks, very few Russians were taken prisoner since Russian propaganda stressed that no-one could expect to survive imprisonment by the Germans. (And indeed, very few did.)

The premature onset of the cold weather in December 1941, and the introduction of the fresh Siberian Divisions, brought the advance on Moscow to a halt. The position in the 'balcony', 80 kilometres from the Soviet capital, grew increasingly difficult for the invaders. The Russians remained fully mobile throughout the winter months.

A Maxim-gun mounted on a simple sledge.

The German paratroopers had to work in the snow with completely inadequate equipment, in temperatures of minus 40 degrees.

Improvisation was vital –
paratroopers became ski troops.

The Russian winter was especially merciless for the maintenance men, the fault-locators. They had to go out at any time, in snow storms and during the most bitter cold, to repair telephone lines destroyed by enemy artillery fire.

Winter equipment was very late in reaching the German front lines. A white jacket with a hood and trousers which could be worn over battle dress offered both warmth and camouflage.

The graves of German soldiers, untraceable today because the
Russians destroyed them.

the front. A scene straight out of the books we have read about the First World War. There are a lot of Russians here too. All of them, male and female alike, are wrapped in a quilted one-piece suit, wearing the same fur hats, the same felt boots. It gives the impression that they were all fresh from the factory. They don't look emaciated at all. On the contrary, they have puffy, well-fed faces and are stocky and averagely tall.

Unfortunately we've no time to see the town itself, so Finner and I go into one of the little houses nearby. We see two women who are fetching water from a nearby spring, then follow them into their house. They are clearly very afraid of us. How poor they are, they have no running water. We have to stoop to get in. On the right there's a goat-stall, smelling dreadfully. The family comes towards us: an old woman, a man in his thirties, a very young woman and three small children. All of them are living in the house, which has just two small rooms. Poorly clothed – without winter wear – they stand in front of us and only become more sociable when we give the old man cigarettes and let them see that we only want to look round. They know an astonishing amount of German and call themselves White Russians. There's even a little Christmas tree here, so some Christianity has kept its hold. The furnishings are miserable, a rough tree-trunk stuck into the ground and draped with a decorated piece of sacking to divide the room. A powerful stove is the biggest piece of furniture in the place. After handing over one or two gifts, we return to the train. Then on to Smolensk. Here and there a German plane flies overhead, and on the few roads we can see endless convoys of cargo transports and Wehrmach vehicles, travelling to and from the front line.

We pass the time playing skat. Later we are shocked to hear that the Staff Waffenfeldwebel, the Technical Sergeant, died in the night – apparently he was sick and choked on his own vomit. We debate amongst ourselves: what does the Commander write to the man's relatives? Does he talk of 'a hero's death for people and fatherland'? Thinking about it can make you feel rotten. Finally we reach Smolensk. It lies in an attractive setting, surrounded by little hills. The town itself, with its numerous church towers, is reminiscent of the period when the Tsar was still the head of the Orthodox Church and the 'Most Christian Emperor'. After all, after the fall of the Roman and Byzantine Churches, the Muscovites regarded Moscow as the third Rome!

A considerable part of the city looks as though it has been destroyed. There must be an airfield at the other side, since planes are constantly landing and taking off. Then we move on into the town, whose name has become famous as a result of the big summer offensive by our troops. Naturally, we recognise the Cathedral, and the embankment our tanks mounted to destroy the enemy positions. At 15.00 hours we stop by the station itself, cheerfully pack our gear together, and wait. The Commander talks with a liaison officer who's trudging around in a heavy fur coat. We're the first unit to get here, and have to await the arrival of the Regiment in a nearby assembly area. We disembark rapidly in the darkness. Silently, and with considerable effort because of the weight of all the gear, the Company marches into the city centre. The men have to sleep together in one large, unheated room in a building that used to be a bank. Well, it'll do for one night. I'm with the other officers over the road in the Hotel Molotov, an imposing building from the outside although architecturally a mess. Resourceful soldiers have stuck stovepipes out of the windows so that they can set up little stoves inside. There is an impressive entrance hall with a wide flight of marble steps, but the three storeys above it have only little corridors and a warren of tiny rooms. Ludicrous really. From the outside a first class Grand Hotel, but inside it's not even third class. No running water, no bath, lousy toilets (we prefer to relieve ourselves in the cold). We've soon had enough, and leave for the Recreation Room for Officers which the nurses have set up. It suddenly occurs to us that today is New Year's Eve, so we get out our last bottles. Tenschert and I visit the men, who are also drinking determinedly. Everything is in order there although, like ourselves, they're all paralytically drunk.

In the morning the Commander is still drinking with some bigwigs and a young holder of the Knight's Cross, whilst I'm busy with the infantry. That night the order comes through for the Battalion to transfer to the Vyasma region. I'm to take three armoured cars and set up advance quarters in four villages north of Vyasma. These are Avlova, Aleshutina, Markova and Senkvina. The Battalion itself will be travelling to Vyasam by air.

Some things go as planned, others don't. In any case, I set off. We wrap ourselves up well against the freezing cold – it must be 40 degrees below – and take straw so that we can take off our shoes and pack our feet to keep them warm.

A clear, brilliant sky. The road is lined with ruined tanks, lorries, burned carts etc., like an avenue but without any trees. The cold forces us to stop frequently to get ourselves warmed up again. Despite all our efforts Fahnenjunker-Feldwebel Gaerts gets frostbite in his toes. After four hours' journey the road eventually branches off to Vyasma, though you can't really call the place a town. Two main roads pass through it, and vehicles of all kinds are passing along them in a continuous stream. It's a real front-line town which makes a powerful impression on us – we're simply not used to seeing infantry assembly areas like this. Vast numbers of boards and signs give details of commands, units and other organisations. Traffic controllers, swathed in thick coats and felt boots, are busy regulating the flow of traffic. We make our way slowly to the station to find out more, but nobody knows anything. Back to the market place. Suddenly, the streets are almost empty and deserted. All the vehicles have careered off into side roads, their occupants gaping up at the sky. High above, a little silver bird is circling, ready to drop its cargo on us. Some bombs are already landing on houses some 150 metres away, but then the flak starts and the aircraft disappears.

Unexpectedly we come across our Commander who's also gone on ahead, and he tells us that the order to transfer here has already been rescinded. Instead we have to set off towards Rzhev – the Russians have broken through there and we're to act as 'fire brigade'. Some prospect. Instead of making a drop in Tiflis – which we expected – we're making for Rzhev, about 80 kilometres from Moscow.

Near the town we wait for the train with Inspektor Bergefeld, so we can guide him in the right direction. Then on full speed ahead, or as quickly as the deep snow will allow. Past Dobino airfield, full of fighter planes. We spend the night of 2/3 January with some of the occupying troops in their little lair, and discover that they are still managing to lead a remarkably comfortable existence. Gaerte has to stay behind in Szystzheva, since his frostbitten feet now look very ugly. Perhaps he'll be spared a worse fate. Then on to Subzov, and it's another thirty kilometres to the front. At Rzhev we have to stop for an hour because of a shortage of fuel, and spend the time watching air attacks. The Russians fly over with impudent bravado and our fighters are far away, out of sight. We ask our way to the airfield, cross the Volga and meet up with units of our own Battalion. We discover that our comrades actually arrived yesterday with the Jus and have already been moved up to the front. They were attacked by two Ratas (slow, light Russian aircraft) and suffered 12 men wounded. There has to be really thick sky up ahead before these can be brought up without hesitation.

Actually I need to rest for another night, but I am desperate to get back to the mob again. So, fill up with petrol and out on the road to Staritza – no easy task, since we can only feel our way forwards in the darkness. We use the least possible amount of light since we're within Russian artillery range here. Through Pilzhev, and now we really have to watch out that we don't land right in the middle of the Russians. There – on the right is the road to Malachova, where the Regimental HQs of Infantry Regiment 18 and Infantry Regiment 58 are based and where our command will be as well. We're greeted by security, as we're now less than three kilometres away from the most advanced line. I report to Oberst von Treskow in the Regimental Command Post.

Our Parachute Machine Gun Battalion, minus 1 Company, is part of Army Group Centre and comes under the command of 16 Infantry Regiment. On the right Infantry Regiment 18, on the left Infantry Regiment 58. Under our command is No. 2 Anti-Aircraft Machine Gun Company, 10 Parachute Assault Regiment and 7 Railway Engineer Company. At 02.00 hours I'm to take a detail and push on to my Company. When I get to the Battalion Command Post I discover that our Company has already been in action, mopping up a wood and then advancing to the Sobakino base. During the action Obergefreite Sommer was killed, Oberfeldwebel Scherer was hit in the upper and lower arm in close combat, and Feldwebele Settele was hit in the head – fortunately only a graze. All of them were brought back to the main casualty station behind the lines. In an old school building, I meet up with around 20 men who have been forced to stay behind due to frostbite. I lie down at once and sleep until woken by the leader of the patrol, an infantry Unteroffizier. He arrives at 01.00 hours, tells me what he's doing and we set wearily off through the snowy moonlit landscape, carrying our heavy gear and wearing our white parkas.

Visibility is excellent for up to 800 metres – but it's the same for the Russians too, unfortunately, and they're reputed to be everywhere in the hinterland. We cross the big Rzhev-Staritza-Moscow motorway into the forest. The men fall silent and trudge along the path in line. Obergefreite Schmidt and Berghammer are having great difficulty dragging their equipment along, but we'll need it at the front. We reach a forest clearing and some barns, and someone hails us softly. The place is an infantry base. Short stop, then on again. We finally emerge from the forest and see the outlines of a village. Past dead Russians, half-buried in the snow and literally frozen stiff. After another half hour we reach the Infantry Battalion Command Post and I'm greeted by the Commander – Hauptmann Wickert. He gives me more directions and we trudge and slither further along the path. For reasons I don't understand, Berghammer has remained behind. We can't wait, so only Obergefreite Schmidt and I go on, through the village. It's uncannily quiet. Then there's a sudden chatter of rifle shots, and we drop flat. It's bloody ridiculous. The company command post must be ahead of us, about 150 metres away. Nothing stirs. The whole thing strikes me as totally idiotic. Surely some sentries must have been posted. At last a figure emerges. It's the guide, sent to direct the troops taking over new positions – and who has apparently shit himself. He leads me to the hut on the far left and reports that I've arrived. I push the door open gladly, hoping for a warm welcome. There's nothing of the kind, though. A mindless, cigarette-smoking crowd is sitting at a table; they give me a funny look, as if to ask what the hell I think I'm doing here. I report to the Company Commander, shake his hand, and have to hand out cigarettes since all theirs are gone. Then I'm given details of the attack and the position. Frankly it looks bloody awful. All the men are fully clothed, and are waiting for the alarm signal which indicates another Russian attack. I'm dog-tired, so I crawl into the corner by a stove and try to get some sleep.

On the morning of 8 January, Oberfeldwebel Lojewski shows me the Company's position, particularly that of my own platoon. The men are tired from the constant watch, but they're still careful. Gröschel's gun is furthest forward and has been set up in a barn. On the far right is Unteroffizier Bernsdorf, one of our best machine-gun squad leaders, close to another barn. On the left of the Company Command Post is a little hollow which is frequently bombarded with harassing fire. Behind it there are two houses in which Unteroffizier Dworak has established himself. At 09.00 the Russians open fire with anti-tank guns and mortars, but soon cease firing. We realise that they're moving into position over there and our howitzer battery chucks some heavy stuff in their direction. After that the day passes uneventfully. The enemy certainly knows who it is they're up against. In the evening Oberleutnant Tenschert arrives for further orders. He's also cursing about this stupid mouse-trap of a position we've been led into. Machine-gunner Peschl from Gröschl's squad is forced to drop out, injured by a backfire which hit him in the arm. At 18.00 hours we receive an order from the Battalion to provide a recce patrol to comb through the country left of the Company Command Post and occupy the barns. I'm assigned for the job with an infantry rifle squad as reinforcement. At 20.00 hours we move out. Oberfeldwebel Lojewski gives us fire suipport with Dworak's gun and Unteroffizier Nienhaus sends a couple of shells over towards the trenches supposedly occupied by the Russians, whilst we burrow slowly through the deep snow. The tracer bullets light up that part of the wood, making a vivid and dramatic impression. The infantry advances on the right, whilst I go with my squad towards the barn, which is lying in the middle of the snowfield. Everything is quiet. Are they just well camouflaged, or have they abandoned their positions? We creep forward, safety catches off our submachine guns. But there's nothing there – and better for us that way.

My group occupies the barn, whilst I go back to make my report. In the meantime Leutnant Leonhardt has arrived. He's to attack at first light and establish contact with the nearby Infantry Regiment, since we're very much in limbo at the moment. I'm to provide fire support along with my men. Dworak's gun is aimed at Serafino, the Scharnagl gun takes over the right side. At 04.00 hours I go out to the two guns to make sure that I've committed the whole situation to memory. Soon after that the Forward Observation Officer arrivs, an Oberleutnant from our heavy battery, and I show him what's involved. The hollow slowly fills up with men from 3 Company, which is being brought up here.

Leutnant Rieke and Feldwebel Schach are in charge of the platoons. The attack has been set for 05.00 hours, but it's already 05.30 and we're still without the artillery support which was supposed to soften up the enemy beforehand. Using the field glasses, we can clearly make out an enemy machine-gun with three men, so we aim one of our heavy machine guns directly at it. Schach's recce patrol, which was sent out to reconnoitre the surrounding countryside, is still missing. Suddenly there's a great burst of fire. It seems that the Russians are shooting from everywhere, though mainly from the right – in the growing daylight, they have certainly noticed that we're preparing to attack. This waiting around is absolutely crazy. The best time for the attack has already passed. The first Russian shells fall well short, but the next land right in the middle of the village. We can make out mortar fire of various kinds, but above all the murderous rattle of the Russian anti-tank guns. In terms of the number of mortars and anti-tank guns, the Russians are far superior to us. Our 'highest leadership' has probably hesitated too long over supplying us with these weapons. We can clearly make out the discharge of the anti-tank gun about 1500 metres away – then wait for the hit. And now he's hit our hollow. Shell after shell comes ripping in, many – thank God – landing short or sailing overhead, and a lot of duds. 3 Company, which had been in position for our planned attack, retreats to the protection of the houses at our rear. One shell lands right in the middle of a group of men, but all of them are able to keep running. By this time I've got back to our barn, from where we can see a group of soldiers approaching the houses in rushes. We're all ready to open fire when we recognise Schach's recce patrol, which we'd given up for lost and had nearly shot to pieces. To cover them we fire off a few rounds into the wood, where we can see large numbers of Russians moving about. Then there's an ear-shattering crack. They've made out where we are and scored a direct hit with a shell on our roof.

Unteroffizier Dworak is screaming dreadfully. His right foot has been almost completely severed below the ankle and is only hanging by a few tendons. Brave Scharnagl has been badly injured too – his right buttock is badly gashed. (In the goods wagon he'll at least be able to lie down, so it won't be so bad.) Quickly we take them below and bed them down carefully in some straw. A medical orderly from 3 Company provides them with makeshift bandages.

Up above, our gunner, Friedl, has stuck to his heavy machine gun and is exchanging fire with the Russians. But suddenly he falls, with a gentle groan. A sharpshooter's bullet has hit him in the head and ended his young life. Now only Gefreite Scholz and I are left up above, but there's no more point in staying up here. We need to set up the machine gun somewhere else.

As Scholz is preparing to pass the machine gun down to me, I seem to see a red fireball about a metre away, then there's a crack and I feel an enormous pain in my right eye. Instinctively I let myself slip to the floor – more shells are falling outside. Scholz has already got his first-aid packet out and bandages me, but now I have to get back for treatment. I reach the nearest tree in one movement, and then I'm forced to crawl along alone. Above me, two shells thud into the trees and cover me with twigs. I'm sweating with the effort of crawling through the snow, cursing foully, as more shells come crashing nearby – as if they were hunting rabbits. The snow is blackened where they have hit. Left alone like that, you find yourself having stupid thoughts. Should I pray? For Christ's sake no: I never needed the Lord before, so I'm not going to bother him now. Go on, go on! Eventually I reach the end of the row of trees and see Suppzewitsch coming towards me. The lad is quite calm – even laughing. He takes me to the dressing station.

On the way we pass soldiers from the Company, who had already given us up for dead when we stopped shooting from our barn. They're delighted that I'm still alive, and I find I can wave back at them, though carefully. At the dressing station I get some proper care at last. They've really got their hands full here, since many of us have been wounded. Soon a sledge arrives, carrying two men who've been badly wounded. Suddenly I realise that I've been weakened by the loss of blood and am totally exhausted, so after another injection of morphine I lie down to sleep. At 22.00 hours a transport leaves for the main casualty clearing station of Plezhki. Our Staff Doctor, May, bids me farewell with good wishes for a speedy recovery, whilst my driver Wohlschläger sends me on my way with cigarettes from his own meagre ration.

The sledge ride takes a bloodly long time, with the two badly wounded men groaning constantly, so I'm thoroughly delighted when we finally reach the clearing station. Enormous activity here as well. Two doctors and a number of orderlies are working at two tables, patching and sawing. The whole room is filled with wounded men from all branches of the armed forces. Soon it's my turn and the doctor tells me that my right eye will have to be removed – I refuse. He goes quickly on to the next man, no time for debate, understandably. An orderly quickly makes me a big turban and I steal away. Leutnant Leonhardt is here as well. His right foot was hit during a counter-attack and his calf has been gashed open. Next to him my excellent comrade in the platoon, Leutnant Tenschert, is sleeping. He's got a bad stomach wound and has no chance of surviving – poor, fine officer. Today the Battalion has suffered many tragic losses, but the position has been held. Wherever paratroopers make their stand, there's no going back. The incredible pride we have simply doesn't allow us to retreat and makes us a legendary force. The others know they can rely on us, so they're delighted when the parachute 'fire-brigade' arrives. It restores their feeling of confidence and security.

I'm restless until I hear that at 01.00 hours two lorries of wounded are to be taken to the military hospital at Rzhev – and then I'm full of beans because I'm on my way. On the way we pass our 2cm anti-aircraft guns, heading for the Front. After a journey lasting several hours we reach the military hospital. I'm careful not to go in – I'm not going to let them cut my eye out without good reason. Instead, I set off to the airfield with an Unteroffizier and a gunner. On the way we pass some wretched infantry units, hobbling along with cloths wrapped round their frostbitten feet. A flight of Ju's arrives, but unfortunately they're going on to Smolensk. So we wait, and wait. At last, at 15.00 hours, some planes leave for Orsa. In we go, along with an Army Inspektor, more paratroopers and some infantrymen. We fly above the enormous forests, flooded countryside, tiny settlements, at a height of 400 metres. It's damned cold again. At least I'm sitting in the radio operator's place on the left, so I can see and I have more room to take off my boots and stick my feet in a blanket. The only way to avoid frostbite is by constant movement and rubbing of your limbs. After four seemingly endless hours we reach the airfield at Orsa. A military ambulance fetches us to the collecting station and then to the military hospital in the town. I'm given fresh bandages there and make the comment that I've only got a graze. The hospital, a very large building with spacious rooms, is superb. We get our rations and I even manage to coax some cigarettes out of the army storekeeper. I must have looked really pathetic to have aroused his sympathy like that ! To my great joy, I meet up with my friend Eugen Scherer, who was to reach the military hopsital in Vienna by train some days later. Unlike me, he wasn't fit to march.

A transport train is due to set off at midnight. No thanks, I know what they're like. I'd rather wait here for an aircraft. The two paratroopeers have already gone out and had an amazing piece of luck: they got one that was heading direct to Erfurt. I'm delighted for them, albeit with a pain in my gut because I can't go with them, dammit. That whole day there are no more aircraft flying in the direction of home. Finally, on 9 January one sets off for Posen, taking us with it. There we're taken to a military hospital, with a kindly senior physician, even nicer Red Cross nurses, hot sweet coffee, slices of sausage. The infantry boys are especially overjoyed – after all, they've been lying out there in the muck for months on end.

I'm only there for a short time. All of us are delighted by our treatment, but then we make our reports and get our marching orders for the journey home. Mine is Posen – Berlin – Munich, which naturally makes me feel absolutely fantastic. But first of all we have to be deloused at the station, every piece of clothing going into a steam-boiler whilst we wash ourselves with a special soap. I hadn't noticed any lice at all but some of the little sods had crept into my clothes – perhaps it was too cold for them outside.

Our train leaves at midnight, so we go off to the tavern at Posen station. I guess we astonished the people there: in our torn, filthy gear, unshaven, we look like real hard cases. The landlord himself appears, clears a good table for us, orders beer to be brought and serves up an enormous roast of venison, almost like at home, as if the Front was thousands of miles away. We're genuinely touched by the comradely welcome from the people of Posen, who bring boxes of cigarettes to our table. They are just ordinary folk people who are travelling by train as well and want to show their compassion for their soldiers. At 02.00 hours the train leaves for Berlin, and we're there by morning. The connection leaves for Munich at 10.00 hours, and after Leipzig I find myself alone in the compartment reserved for the wounded and can really stretch out. It's a very special feeling to be travelling home to my parents and loved ones: they've no idea where I've been posted and even less that I've been wounded.

We arrive in Munich at 23.00 hours and I manage to catch the last slow train to Ottobrunn. Nobody in the train recognises me in my paratroopers' gear, plus a heavy overcoat stuffed with cigarettes, cigars and a bottle of booze, my hair awry, head bandage filthy, and no cap. My parents have long since gone to bed, but I know where the key is kept. I call upstairs so they won't be frightened, and then they fold me in their arms. Of course, I have to explain the wheres, whys and wherefores, but soon I'm sinking into my own white bed. It's a long time before I can sleep, though – my thoughts keep returning to events at the front and to my comrades there.

On the next morning – 11 January – I go into the city. The hospitals are full to overflowing, but eventually I'm transferred by the Oberföhring Luftwaffe Hospital to the University Eye Clinic. Although it's almost 18.00 hours by now, the nurses make me welcome and put me into bed, and soon I'm on the operating table. An injection in the eyelid for local anaesthetic, then the senior physician mutters 'I can save the eye'. He uses forceps to remove a fragment from my right eye and then, from behind the eyeball, an extremely dented small arms bullet. I'm astonished at my good fortune. Out there I would have lost my eye, but here it was saved by a superb eye specialist. Unbelievable. From 12 January until 28 February I stay in Oberföhring. After 14 days I can even start admiring the girls again once those deeply fascinating bandages are finally removed. On 28 February I get my orders to set out for 1st Parachute Replacement Regiment in Stendal. My first Russian campaign was a short one and soon over, but already I'm looking forward to more action. But this time, I hope, by parachute!

On Stand-by in the West

(From 16.9.1942 to 3.10.1942 we came under the command of 7th Airborne Division, acting as mobile Division of the Reserve Army Group of Field Marshal von Rundstedt, Commander of the Army in the West. A second rear position was being prepared here in case of a British invasion. The Parachute Machine Gun Battalion was placed under the command of 7th Airborne Division and had its quarters in the Saint Sever – Villedeu sector of the Departement Calvados.)

We're still at the Grossborn troop training grounds and there's been great activity for days as we know we're being transferred to France. On one hand it's a pity, since our new young recruits urgently need a few more weeks of really hard training. On the other hand it should be a bit of a holiday camp, since we can take all our stuff with us. As if it's a matter of course, I'm appointed loading officer yet again. On 17 September we load up and set off, after two years almost to the day, back to France again. Accompanied by Oberleutnant Klitzing and Regimental Inspektor Berkefeld, I divide up the compartments. Next door is Hauptmann Laun with Inspektor Finner. It's true about a holiday camp outing, since I've even got my little table for playing skat. Quite incredible.

Berlin – Hanover – Neuss-on-Rhine. Here you can see a lot of ruined houses, and others which have had new roofs put on. Then through the huge Belgian industrial region to Namur, which we reach at 16.40 hours. On the way, many of the names remind us of the battlefields of the First World War. For a while we travel along the Seine, by midday we're in Versailles, by evening in Argentan and at 01.00 hours in Saint Sever. We manage to disembark quickly until, for no apparent reason, two wagons tip over on the tracks and we have difficulty unloading the gear.

We draw up in front of the town hall in the morning, singing loudly. It's an attractive little town, picturesquely situated beneath a hill. We're welcomed by the leader of the advance party, Oberfeldwebel Knäble, who hands out the billeting order. I'm welcomed by friendly, middle-class people who immediately offer me a snack. A pleasant room with a wide French bed reminds me of home and my reserve batman Obergefreite Schröder quickly gets down to work. At mealtimes we usually go to the 'Moderne' Hotel, or to the 'Normandie'. There's still an abundance of food here, the fried potatoes swimming in fat, the butter spread centimetres thick and gorgeous fruit on the bedside table – peaches, and grapes by the pound. As our saying goes, in France you can live like a god.

There's great activity in the towns. According to reports from our spies, a million soldiers are massed on the southern coast of England, ready to invade the Continent. Currently there is high-tide in the Channel, making it a favourable period for an Allied landing. The Regiments have bivouacked on the coast, whilst we're to act as Division reserve – excellent!

If called up, we could be thrown into action in Holland, or as far south as the Spanish frontier. Perhaps things will hot up for us again quite soon. Equipment, weapons and ammunition are all kept ready so that we'll be ready to move within an hour.

But nothing happens, so we have to stave off boredom by means of field exercises. For the first time, we see the difficulties which both the attackers and the defenders (ourselves) will have to contend with here. The countryside consists of little plots of land with high hedges around, and deep hollows – any fighting here is bound to be bitter. But for now things are quiet, and our first packs of butter are despatched homewards. In the evenings by the fireside, rumours begin to circulate: there's not going to be an invasion, we'll be going back east.

In fact, on 1 October our Company entrains with Oberleutnant von Pretzmann, whilst Hauptmann Laun and I are to follow with the rest. We spend the next day on a shopping trip to Vire, with my Feldwebel Gaerte providing useful assistance through his famous command of French.

Leonhardt, Ruthe and Kanthak Companies are already entraining, with us to follow tomorrow.

In the afternoon of 13 October we move out, together with Inspektor Jost, Oberarzt Schrödinger, Hauptmann Laun and Oberleutnant Meinke. Once again we enjoy a comfortable journey through the beautiful countryside. Only as we reach Düsseldorf do we start to feel anxious – from then on, for kilometre after kilometre on both sides of the railway, the houses have been burned and destroyed. In the main station every single window is broken, and the Church has been burned down as well. It looks terrible, like the

East. But some day our Luftwaffe will fly over England's cities, and God help that island then. This is the only idea that comforts us when we see what has happened here. In my case, this spiritual unease is aggravated by a violent case of the shits, which forces me to take up more or less permanent residence in the bog.

On 16 October we're back in our old garrison town of Gardelegen. Now it looks as though we'll be in action again soon. Maybe, we hope, the parachute drop for which we've waited so long.

Russia 1942/3 – Central Sector

(Here I'm relying on Sergeant-Major Wild's war diary, telling me that we had been ordered back to Russia by 19 October.) This time we're to be sent to the Welisz-Surasz-Demidorff region, which means that we aren't to make a drop but are to act as mobile 'fire brigade' again. We regard ourselves as a unit of elite troops, but they are apparently determined to send us to the slaughter in infantry operations. Oh yes, the news has certainly spread that when the paratroopers arrive, the front holds.

From 4 Regiment, Leutnant Stahl of 3 Company is put under our command, along with Obergefreites Nagel, Fuchs, Wald and Fried from the communication section. On 7 November we move into position on the Szappszo Lake. In my platoon, calm and reliable Feldwebel Sulima is leading 1 Group and Feldwebel Gaerte 2 Group, but he's soon transferred to headquarters personnel as an officer candidate. My platoon headquarters leader is Unteroffizier Hein.

The first weeks are spent building bunkers, communication trenches, camouflaged machine gun positions, the installation of sledge paths for supplies etc. Up above in the Company Command Post, they're even building a sauna. Our tireless old organiser Hauptmann Laun is really in his element. After a long time, I've at last got decent skis under my feet again, enabling me to travel cross-country to Kiselli and the supply train.

These are quiet days, with only a few salvoes of rifle and machine-gun fire from the Russians on the islands over on the other side. Perhaps because of this, an incomprehensible laxity has made its appearance in the Company. Protected by the lake, the men reckon that they are quite safe here. When I return from a patrol of our positions, the sentry fails to notice me until I'm within three metres of him. If I'd been the enemy, he'd be dead. At another of our positions, nicknamed 'Cape Horn', both sentries have made themselves comfortable: Gefreite Stöger is lying fast asleep, in the full light of day. Maybe he already guessed that on 10 December he'd be seriously wounded by a bullet through the head.

Our embrasures are too widely spaced and have to be altered. I've got the power to grant leave for three men, but wonder seriously whether I shouldn't refuse to let them go, since the attitude of the men in general has been so unsatisfactory. But then, we're so far from home, and our loved ones are waiting for us.

On 14 December we come under heavy mortar fire and, despite our excellent positions, Gefreite Zweig receives a serious head wound, Obergerfreite Langer is shot through the upper arm shortly afterwards, and Gefreite Beckert is hit by shell splinters. Yet despite these casualties, the men will only work when I arrive on the scene and make them. They must know how important for their own safety it is to build secure positions, but they're as stubborn as mules, totally pigheaded. There are excellent fellows among them, but many are revealing their bad sides. This criticism includes our NCOs, the Unteroffiziere, as well. What infuriates me most is that they've suddenly forgotten how to improvise, so that everything has to be decided for them and orders given before they'll do anything. The most reliable man is still Feldwebel Sulima.

In mid-December it gets dreadfully wet and cold, snow and rain together. The Russians will soon have to withdraw from the furthermost islands, so they won't be so close. But we're in mire up to our knees!

And then suddenly there's a cloudless, starlit night, a wonderful blue morning sky. Unfortunately, along with it comes the onset of the most appalling, biting cold. At least we're better equipped for this second Russian winter, with thick overcoats, felt boots, earflaps, parkas. We content ourselves with providing intermittent but effective concentrations of fire, particularly with our mortars and 3.7cm anti-tank guns. Otherwise it stays quiet. Von Pretzmann celebrates with us, in no uncertain manner, the birth of his second daughter – not a dry eye in the house. An amazing drunken session, followed by a hangover of equally enormous proportions. Then post arrives from home and, naturally enough, the mood of the men improves. My fiancée encloses a photograph and my batman carves a lovely frame for it out of beechwood.

We're preparing our wartime Christmas and are rewarded with a heavy fall of snow. In the early morning the area roundabout has become like something out of a fairytale. The branches are bending under the weight of the snow, and glittering like sugar-covered Christmas cakes. Quickly off with the skis and off for a general clean-up in the sauna, down 'to the last louse'. A fantastic bath, leaving me feeling wonderfully fit and well. But then another piece of bad luck. We've scarcely finished celebrating the arrival of Obergefreite Demitter when our gunner Krin is wounded. We still have hardly enough men to post proper sentries so men have to be sent to us from the train – at least they're good paratroop drivers.

Naturally enough, the whole place is in chaos on the 24 December. For days the men have been making attractive decorations and ornaments such as lamps, ashtrays, and picture frames, and have been putting up Christmas trees and decorating them with silver foil from our cigarette packets. In the morning Ivan leaves us in peace, but he spends the afternoon shooting aimlessly throughout the whole area. It's clear that the Commissars want to spoil our Christmas celebrations if they can. Unchristian of them, and doomed to be unsuccessful.

Early in the evening I take a detachment from the platoon to the Commander. Each base has made a little present for him – for instance the 'Cape of Good Hope' has made a beautiful lamp and 'Cape Arcona' a litter basket. The Commander is very enthusiastic about these gifts and spends a short time celebrating the festive season with us. For Christmas each officer receives some spirits, twenty cigars, forty cigarettes etc., and the men get similar gifts. We return to the bunker with a sledge crammed with letters and presents for the men. From far away we can here them singing Christmas carols, the harsh deep voices of the older men and the light tones of the youngest soldiers, our newest recruits. We're greeted joyously, and deliveries are taken to all the sentries and to every base. A real festive mood takes hold.

It's my first real wartime Christmas. I'm up again very early on Christmas morning, first of all to attend to my duties, collating and evaluating the reports. But then I can attend to my own parcels, stuffed with cigarettes, delicious biscuits, pralines and chocolate. Although the sausage has somehow got mixed up with the apples and pralines, it's still the best I've ever tasted. Each letter is read over and over again, each man alone with his feelings. Of course, Ivan sends his own special Christmas greetings in the form of 12cm shells and little 7.62 'cigars', but the bunkers we worked so arduously to build prove themselves strong and secure, and the Russians can't spoil our good humour.

On the 26 December – when I'm still at Company HQ with two of my men – we spot a red alarm signal from below. Red alert! We race pell-mell back to base. More signals – white this time – illuminate the night sky, sub-machine guns crack, we can hear rifle and the more gentle pop of pistols. Within twenty minutes, we reach our little peninsula. The Russians have made their way over the ice with a raiding party of about twenty men and have attacked our island. Yet again, the sentries didn't see them until too late. But my men were on their toes this time and responded so effectively that I almost missed the action altogether.

We scour the entire base, shooting at the Russians in their white parkas as they try to escape on foot and on skis. Between 10 and 15 of them are lying some twenty to fifty metres away, not moving, apparently dead. But when one of my men goes closer, he's shot (though fortunately only wounded slightly). To avoid any further casualties on our side, I make several calls for the Russians to surrender; when they don't, I order the men to fire on each and every one. Only then do we approach them. There are no Commissars among them. They're carrying sludgy bread in their haversacks, also millet, and are mostly Asiatics, well-nourished and wearing practical winter clothing.

After that things are quiet for a time, but then from 18.30 until 19.15 hours the Russians bombard the entire sector with machine-gun and mortar fire, at least three barrels of 7.62 artillery. Gefreite Horn is wounded by a shell splinter in the thigh. Our own artillery returns the fire, managing to silence the enemy guns. Our telephone lines have been cut, so the line-layers have to brave the cold night to retrieve the situation.

Until New Year everything stays nice and peaceful, with only a Russian field gun giving us cause to scuttle hither and thither. Ivan brings this into the front line before daybreak, fires a couple of times and then disappears again. The Russians have an impressive superiority over us in heavy guns and are damned impressive at finding the range. Back in officer training school we'd been told about the superb Russian artillery skills and the fact that they had entire battalions of the stuff. Why didn't our side take account of it and set up heavy artillery battalions of our own? What we have is nowhere near enough.

New Year's Eve (This is what I wrote at the time):

The men are sitting at the tables, recounting stories about the year gone by, talking about the action we've seen and the many friends we've lost. Although there's plenty of punch and grog the mood remains quiet. Five minutes before midnight each man lifts his glass, and we drink quietly and calmly to the New Year. What will it bring us? Our thoughts and conversations turn towards home, to our loved ones, our Führer and our Fatherland.

We're not afraid to cry as we stand to remember our Führer and our fallen comrades. It's like an oath binding us together, making us grit our teeth and carry on until victory.

What is life worth to us? It's true that our joy in living and lust for life are stronger now than they've ever been, but each of us is ready to sacrifice his life for the holy Fatherland. This Fatherland is my faith, and my only hope. All the best feelings in my heart are directed towards it.

At home, they'll be sitting under the Christmas tree as well. I can see my brave old Dad, see him stand and drink with reddened eyes to the soldiers. And my courageous mother, she'll certainly be crying a bit, and my little sister too. But one day there'll be another New Year when we can all be together, happily reunited after a victorious end to the mass slaughter of the nations. That superior spirit which moves the young people must lead us to victory: there is no alternative. To win through or to die in battle – those are my thoughts at 01.00 hours on the first day of 1943.

Now, forty years later, as I sit and look at these notes I wrote then, I can only shake my head in wonder at the way our young people were so inspired, but so very much misled. And I want to shout, to cry out to the youngsters of today: Never, never let yourselves be persuaded into fighting for anyone or anything. Yet still I must admit to doubts, to the feeling that under certain circumstances it might be necessary to risk one's life to protect freedom.

But then – what is freedom?

We toil and labour at our bunkers and defensive positions, for it seems certain that the Russian's big attack won't be delayed much longer and they'll certainly attempt to blow us all to pieces beforehand. On 7 January Gefreite Timm is hit in the lower body, and Erken has a dangerous stomach wound. Then Rochlitz accidentally shoots himself, in the head, whilst cleaning his pistol. The men are drilled over and over again, and instructed to take extra care when cleaning their weapons, but these things still happen. Fate.

On 11 January I order my men to cease fire – maybe it'll make Ivan a little nervous about our intentions.

We're still desperately short of men, enough to make us celebrate the arrival of every replacement. On 12 January Gefreite Dietrich arrives, fresh from Gardelegen. This damned work and the continuous watchfulness are really playing on our nerves. But only a couple of hours later, Obergefreite Wilfert is brought in with a head wound. The irregular Russian zone fire continues to claim its victims, and we're powerless against it despite taking every precaution.

On 14 January there's another large delivery of post, which cheers everyone up no end. Although the days remain quiet, at night the Russians have started sending over large numbers of reconnaissance planes. Something's definitely in the air. Horn arrives from the military hospital, and we're sent Gefreites Balz and Hansen from the train. A bit of breathing space at last. Then my old platoon headquarters leader, Unteroffizier Dewitz, arrives back from officer candidate school. Oberleutnant Hölters has been killed in action and I go on my skis to his funeral. But then I get an unexpected pleasure when I meet up with my old gunner from Dietl gun, Max Grübl, and he's got the most enormous parcel for me. My sweet innocent parents have given it him to bring for me – they obviously think that you can travel right up to the front line by train.

Old 'Iron Gustav' is still circling around, we see it almost every day on its reconnaissance flights. We've no anti-aircraft guns so it goes its way unhindered. Obergefreite Götz has been wounded. But we're managing to harass the Russians too, from our strongly built and well-camouflaged defensive positions, with fixed fire from our machine-guns. We already know where they are and can adjust our fire accordingly. I manage to get someone from a range of 1400 metres.

One afternoon I narrowly escaped a flight of my own. Quite unsuspectingly, I was standing near an explosive charge unaware that it was about to be detonated. A sudden shout of 'Get down!' and I fell flat just as the whole lot went up. Fortunately for them, the shock made me completely forget to shoot the idiots on guard.

Since 1 February we've been in a state of increased alert: according to information from Russian deserters, the big offensive will begin on my right flank. There are also rumours that we're to be relieved – many even purport to know the exact date. But such stories leave the veterans amongst us cold, we're immune to latrine rumours by now.

Unteroffizier Idzykowski is firing at a Russian sentry post using the telescopic sight, observed by Obergefreite Fuchs and myself. Suddenly there's a hail of fire from the other side. When Fuchs grabs himself around the heart I'm sure that he's done for and start to drag him to the trenches. But he manages to hobble to the bunker under his own steam – I can hardly believe my eyes – and removes a 14 milimetre antitank rifle bullet from his shoe! We're both stunned at his incredible luck. At 11.00 hours Obergerfeite Waldfried is hit at the entrance to the bunker. Though I get to him straight away, there's nothing anyone can do to save him. At least his death means that he was spared a court-martial for his serious misconduct and dereliction of duty during his sentry duties. Unfortunately, incidents such as those are greatly on the increase at the moment. I catch Obergefreite Kluwe with a woollen scarf wrapped round both ears during sentry duty, having got within two metres of him. I'd really like to give him a good military thrashing. This negligence, it's enough to make you puke!

5 February. Stalingrad is on everybody's lips. We try to imagine what the soldiers there must be enduring, and marvel at their heroic dedication to duty. Surely their conduct will strengthen our whole people – a nation which has such men can never be defeated.

In the middle of February the thaw sets in – and how! Now we can clearly see the enemy's trenches and bunkers, and they can see ours just as plainly. Water is dripping and running everywhere; the mud is knee-deep in the trenches and has to be shovelled out; clothes and weapons are all filthy.

19 February. It's 02.00 hours. I can't get the Goebbels speech calling for total war out of my mind. The speech was so tremendous and fantastic that I feel I have to write home with my own response. Everyone was carried away by his words, all of us were under his spell. He spoke to us from the heart. Total War at last – yes of course, but why not earlier? He calls for the utmost effort from each and every one of us, for each one to do his duty in service to the Fatherland. Only in this way – we all agree – can we win the war. For us, Stalingrad was a signal, calling us to make a sacred commitment.

20 February. One of my best men, Max Grübl, has been killed in a place where hardly any other shots were fired, by a bullet through the collar bone which pierced a blood vessel. His young, strong life has been snuffed out. A fine lad, through and through. He would have been the first to be granted leave, in recognition of his guts in the counter-attack on 'Cape Horn'. – We're going to miss him, our Max.

Yesterday I came back from a tour round the Front. I made an enormous cross-country ski trip via Kiselli-Sabolotze-Klimati to Oberleutnant Ruthe's 'game park'. They're living in feudal conditions there, in the best of senses, in a giant 'bungalow' made of birchwood with an open chimney and chairs of birch. Misloviky, Eugen Scherer, the 'Cap'n' and all the old Feldwebels were there, so we got drunk on memories and current happenings as well as on vast quantities of alcohol. After long abstinence I was so totally plastered that I took days to get over it. Those were two wonderful days, unforgettable. I met up with Kay Umbach again, a man I remembered from the old days. A nice chap and very much on the ball when things needed organising, he had important connections. Once he was told to acquire wine in the Rhineland and was given six days to do it. Without informing anybody, he took twelve days before appearing with large quantities of wine, and simply said that it couldn't be done any quicker. Whenever he went and did something wrong, he just called his uncle in the Reich Air Ministry in Berlin, General Christiansen, and everything was hunky-dory. He had an excellent relationship with Oberleutnant Ruthe. This gentleman was a young huntsman and Kay managed to organise many a fine hunt for them both. I was astonished at the superb supplies and the vast quantities of schnapps they'd acquired. A few weeks later, however, I discovered that he and Ruthe had definitely gone too far. As it was described to me, a rations supply bunker had already been set up in no man's land for a future advance. Kay managed to track it down, with the approval of Ruthe, and they were living in the land of milk and honey on the contents. It was obvious that they had things that we could only dream about – we hadn't had any stuff like that for ages. But then the whole thing was discovered and this time even Kay had to take at least some of the blame. Both men were transferred.

25 February. Slowly but surely, life is changing. Most of the winter clothing has been withdrawn. Gefreite Haas, wounded two weeks ago by a bullet in the leg, comes back to us. Sadly for him, he hadn't got a nice 'blighty' one this time.

A variety show at the train in Sachoti. A Ukrainian troupe in attractive national costume puts on a really excellent performance, wonderful folk-dances to Russian music. It was well worth the hour-long march to get there. Things are still quiet, with only our 'Knallmax' gun firing to great effect at the Russian bunkers. In the evening we visit the Commander to discuss the general situation, and also to talk lightheartedly about job training. Fred Kröger suggests that we should build a house together, me as manager and him as cook. (He reminded me about the conversation years later, and we had a good laugh over it).

On 10 March I order the platoon to fire at will – six heavy machine guns, two light machine guns and a number of mortars. A superb piece of theatre as the tracer trajectories cut through the night sky, it really cheered the men up. Five Russian Martin bombers fly overhead, but fortunately they drop their cargo well behind us. Since yesterday there has been no firing at all from the islands opposite. Has Ivan evacuated the area, or is he just trying to make us think so? The footbridge to my command post, fifty metres long and one metre fifty wide, is finished, well-camouflaged and only waiting for its official opening. Now I've been promoted to 'Prince of the Szappszo Lake' and anyone who passes by has to pay tribute. The days are becoming more beautiful, warmer, the nights are clearer and we don't need to post as many sentries.

On 20 March the great battle begins. From 05.15 hours the Russian artillery has been firing in our left sector. Within a few minutes at least two hundred shells from twelve gun barrels have been counted, along with 7.62, 10.5 and 12cm mortars. A sinister rolling barrage across the Front. Nine Ratas fly over Tinovka, and at the same time the Russian artillery is firing smoke grenades in the direction of Akti, certainly as a signal. My Idzykowski recce patrol arrives back and runs into Oberleutnant Leonhardt, who's taking his platoon to reinforce the Gustmann's Hill. But no enemy movement can be seen, at least not where we are. Close by on our left, though, we hear that seven or eight tanks have broken through, and two assaults by Russian infantry have been beaten off. Along the entire enemy line we can hear loud voices, the barking of dogs, the noise of lorries and tanks. On the next day there's another heavy barrage, this time up to 18cm calibre, four 'Stalin organs' (Katyusha multi-barrelled rocket projectors) with them: these have little effect but their eerie whistling stretches the nerves to breaking point. The fire is getting too close and I order the reserve group to get ready, Feldwebel Sulima with fourteen men. The bombardment continues to increase, but at last our own artillery is returning fire. At 10.45 hours the news comes in that Maklakova has been retaken in a counter-attack. Eventually, things quieten down. The Russians haven't achieved the breakthrough. They were facing 4 Regiment over there, commanded by the excellent Commander Walter, a man I know from Narvik.

Nothing happens after all, so on 25 March the old rumours about a transfer return start circulating again. Where will we be sent?

Damn it, at least let's get away from here. We're attack troops, not defenders.

There was a lot of action last night. At 22.00 hours our own artillery began a bombardment of the 'Knobloch' base, to such effect that windows here rattled and the sand trickled through the joists. For two solid hours they bombarded the positions in order to soften them up. At 04.00 hours the base was seized back from the Russians with very few casualties on our side.

The rumours that we're about to be relieved have proved to be well-founded. At 16.00 hours officers from the relief unit come through the positions. The 'Murderers Division' – we don't know why they're called that – is relieving us, excellent infantrymen. Two of their Hauptmanns with the Gold Cross are discussing the situation with us. Then on 28 March it actually happens. At 02.30 hours the sentry suddenly shouts in delight: 'The relief is here!' You had better believe how happy we are. Our base is taken over by a Leutnant with a heavy machine-gun squad, its Unteroffizier a fine East Prussian and an excellent marksman.

There's no question of sleep now so we chat until morning. Then it's time to guide the new men round our positions, hand over sketches and situation maps, count ammunition and hand it over, and finally make our departure. 'Cape Horn' and 'Pigheaded Bunker' have been our home for six months, half a year full of happenings. The long nights of entrenchment, the work, the watching – they're all over now. I think of our many wounded and of our dead comrades Max Grübl, Zweig and Waldfried, men we must leave in this place.

We march along the filthy, swampy roads for twenty-five kilometres, seeing columns of vehicles, detachments of men marching to the Front or – like ourselves – back from it. At 16.00 hours we reach Bonokovo, our objective for the day, and squeeze into houses which are already full to bursting, hoping at least to warm our chilled bodies at a warm stove.

Next day I go with Schmitz, Schröder, Minth and Kissel as an advance party to Demidoff and get some Russians to prepare a couple of houses for the men. Then I'm in another advance party to Rudnija, about forty-seven kilometres, lucky that we don't have to go on foot. A flash of inspiration takes me to the station and, yes, in the afternoon an empty train is due to leave for Vitevsk. I keep on and on until they agree to wait, and the train takes the Company with it. We race ahead to Vitevsk and discover that we're to go to our old area in

Russia 1942/3

Rest during the advance in the Welilisz-Surasz-Demidoff region at the beginning of
November 1942. Standing, from left: Oberleutnant Hirsch, Oberleutnant von
Pretzmann and Leutnant Pöppel.

In October 1942 the Machine Gun Battalion returned to Russia to reinforce the defensive line on the hard-pressed central sector. The Red Army had concentrated four predominantly Siberian Divisions here in the hope of achieving the breakthrough. The battle lasted for months, with the German troops well-entrenched in excellent bunkers and at last with winter equipment enabling them to tolerate temperatures of 40 degrees below zero more easily.

Leutnant Martin Pöppel.

View from the 'pigheaded' bunker over the frozen Szappszo Lake. The approaches
were thinly defended with mines.

Hauptfeldwebel Wild on the way to
inspect the advanced positions.

A typical bunker, comfortable and well-camouflaged, containing warm bunks made of birch trunks and straw mattresses.

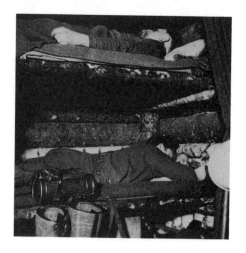

Feldwebel Sullima (left) and Unteroffizier Idzykowski (centre) during the construction of the bunker.

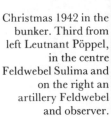

Christmas 1942 in the bunker. Third from left Leutnant Pöppel, in the centre Feldwebel Sulima and on the right an artillery Feldwebel and observer.

On inspection. From left: Hauptmann Laun, Stabsarzt Dr. Puppel, Leutnant Pöppel and Oberleutnant Hirsch.

Transporting the wounded with horse-drawn sledges.

On 28 March we were relieved by the infantry. Back through the muddy roads, 25 kilometres to Bonokovo and then on again to Babinitszi. In the right foreground is Gefreite Kai Umbach.

1 Machine Gun Company as guests in Bayreuth. From left: Unteroffizier E. A. Müller, Hauptfeldwebel Wild, Oberfeldwebel Wilhelm Lojewski (with Spain Cross), Mr Eberhard, Technical Director of the Bayreuth Festivals (in light-coloured suit), and (far right) Oberfeldwebel Misoviky.

Rear party detachment of the Machine Gun Battalion in Gardelegen under Leutnant Kade from III/1.

Babinitszi. We stay a few days and get our equipment into some sort of order. We reckon that we're sure to be heading for France. Could it be that we'll be off to Argentan again?

On 3 April I get the whole Company and its vehicles entrained and we set ourselves up in the goods carriages. 'We' – that is the 1 Parachute Machine Gun Battalion and the members of the antitank unit with the self-propelled guns. At 19.00 hours we pass Minsk, then through endless marshlands, fallow land, vast forests. As we're about to hang up our hammocks to sleep there's an explosion, the smell of gunpowder, splinters of wood and coal. the train stops. Light out, weapons at the ready. A mine has exploded under our carriage and torn it apart. Of the men of 1 Platoon, Ebert has been badly wounded, Bader, Reichert, Schuster, Stolpke and Gumpoltsperger less seriously. We seal the place off and stand on guard, then fetch engineers from the locomotive. It's our good fortune that a hospital train is just arriving which can take our wounded.

The journey continues through Brest-Litovsk, Radom, Warsaw. Young kids are swarming about the station here, trading in every possible kind of goods. Their chocolate turns out to be biscuit with a coating, their trashy letter paper is expensive as hell. Much laughter as the station police arrive, confiscate the goods and distribute them to the troops.

We notice a great deal of construction and building work in the Warthegau (translator's note: the area of western Poland annexed by Germany). Then into the Reich itself, where we recognise German thoroughness, cleanliness and order, the streets full of well-dressed people and the girls already in light clothes.

Glogau, Halle – we still don't know where we're bound. It's now 8 April and real April weather – it's snowing.

Among the new railway crew is a confirmed Communist from Cassel who has skat cards instead of a prayer book. He was sent to a concentration camp in 1933, fled to the Soviet Union in 1934 in order to find the justice he was seeking but was banished in 1937 (no-one knew why). Some people were shot and others fled, like himself. So he returned to the Reich, cured of his love for the Workers' Paradise. In simple language, he tells us his story. We won't forget it, not for a long time.

Cassell, Coblenz, Trier. Then delousing in Moumelon on 10 May. We find ourselves sitting in a large, well-heated room, from gunners through to the Hauptmann, all together for the first time in ages. To celebrate we have a singing competition, and a lot of laughs.

Paris, along the Seine once again, Chartres and Alancon where the anti-tank men disembark so they can travel on to Bouce. But we're staying here. Feldwebel Krassa arrives and there's much to tell. At the Hotel 'La France' I discover first-class private quarters and we're greeted by M. Demorell, who owns a local laundry business. A couple of wonderful days there, then I'm ordered to report to the Commander.

Fantastic news! I'm to return to Gardelegen as officer in charge of the rear party detachment. Four whole weeks in the Reich, four weeks with Gerda, my girl. I set off on Maundy Thursday and arrive home on Easter Saturday. 'Home' – in this case, meaning our garrison town of Gardelegen.

Sicily 1943

After our return from Russia we were originally moved to St Chamas in southern France, and then to Senas in the same region, where we remain. For weeks now there have been daily exercises to prepare against enemy operations by land and air. The whole world is waiting for the Anglo-American invasion of Europe – the only thing is, nobody knows where it will come. But there's a strong possibility that the first drama will be played out in the south.

Over and over again, weapons containers are packed at top speed and embarkation exercises perfected. Scarcely a night goes by without us being turfed from our beds to improve our combat readiness. We officers have two sleeping quarters. In normal conditions we're housed very comfortably in French villas, but when we're put on stand-by by the Division and told to maintain combat readiness, then we have to pitch camp in the old barracks.

These constant alerts eventually have a dulling effect, since after a while nobody really thinks that they'll ever come to anything. So I'm not particularly impressed when my batman races in at crack of dawn to wake me. In full combat gear, I wait until a Company messenger thunders in to tell me to report immediately to Battalion HQ. Now that's not an everyday summons, so I pause long enough to throw a few things together, especially tobacco. It's bloody freezing at this hour of the morning and I'm a bit uneasy about what lies ahead.

I report to the Commander, who immediately sends me as an officer courier to the Division at Cavallion, with a number of questions. Something's definitely afoot, the other alerts weren't like this. We soon reach the town by motorcycle. With some amusement, I think back to the officers' cooking course that was set up here by order of General Heidrich. Utterly untalented in this area, I only managed to produce a few tomatoes, filled with a diced meat salad (and even that had been made by other people), although I must say that the whole thing was rather cleverly garnished. After my attempts at breadmaking, all that was left in the mess tin was an undefinable dumpling of cement.

Now the atmosphere is very different as we wait for the Staff Major. At 06.30 hours all the couriers have arrived and we're ushered in to see Oberst Häring, 1 General Staff Officer of the Division. We stand round the map table, pencil and map at the ready. Big disappointment. We're not told anything about the situation or the operation in prospect, only that all units must prepare for a parachute drop. At least that news cheers us up. There are rumours of an overland flight of 6000 kilometres with an intermediate landing in Italy. That could mean Greece, Italy or even Crete. Now that would be best of all, if the Anglos had landed *there* again, on the island we conquered two years ago. Then we deal with the battle groups and the departure airfields, and return to base. In camp, everything has been prepared for the departure. The motor transport columns have been moved up and camouflaged. The vehicles are lined up, well apart, on a broad highway guarded by tall poplars.

Hauptmann Hirsch is to bring the train overland to Rome. A pity for him, he'd have enjoyed some action. Later, I discovered something that I still find absolutely incredible. Gefreite Otto Porr, horse handler for Major Schmidt, has been given the job of bringing his three mounts along. We appear to be fighting a feudal war!

The field kitchens are steaming, and long lines of soldiers are queuing for their hot tea with rum. Afterwards, to comply with the new orders, uniforms are changed and the companies modified. It's quickly done, and then we wait for the order to pull out.

At 15.00 hours the order eventually reaches us by radio to transfer immediately to Airfield Orange at Avignon. The columns form up, and the Battalion gets under way. Meanwhile, we've heard over the radio that the Allies have invaded Sicily. Now our prospects are clear. It looks like our company is going into action there with a combat strength of two officers and 90 NCOs and other ranks. The others are on leave, have been seconded elsewhere, or are on the notorious Heydrich courses. We reach the airfield by evening, but as there's no prospect of a flight that day we pitch camp and eat. The airfield itself is choc-a-bloc with aircraft, He-111s, He-126s, our old friend Aunti Ju-52 and a whole armada of gliders – all ready for take-off. They're well camouflaged, lying round the perimeter of the airfield or hidden in nearby copses. With luck, we'll be away in the morning. The mood among the men is fantastic at the prospect of more action at last, and maybe even a parachute drop.

11 July. We slept excellently under the aircraft until woken by the sunshine on our faces. The sky is a beautiful azure blue, the sunlight already dazzling. Not necessary to wash, anyway where would we get water? The whole morning is spent in preparation, loading the weapons containers into the aircraft bomb-racks. But it's clear that we're short of at least ten aircraft and the Commander, quite rightly, is reluctant to let his battle group be broken up. It's got damned hot, with the sky itself shimmering in the glare of the sun, even under the shadow of the aircraft. This time we're not going to be transported in the old Jus, by the way, but in the stylish He-111s.

I write one more letter to my girl, telling her about these last moments. She'll already suspect where I am, because where else would I be likely to be with an operation like this going on? We eat lunch in a little canteen that's been erected, with a schnapps or two afterwards, to wash it down. Then it's 16.00 hours and – almost incredibly – the order for take-off has finally arrived. On with life-jackets, a last few photographs, then into the aircraft with many handshakes for those left behind. Strap on the belts, though I move forwards into the nose compartment. Take-off at 17.00 hours. The propellers turn faster and faster, the engines roar into life, and the surface wind churns up the dust, throws it high into the air. The first aircraft roll to the runway, take off and soar away. Then it's our turn. Still nobody knows exactly where we're heading, not even the pilots themselves. They have a sealed envelope which they've only allowed to open at a specific stage of the flight. But we know it now.

(After the landing of the Anglo-American forces on Sicily, 1 Parachute Division, stationed in southern France as Armed Forces High Command Reserve, was transferred there with the greatest possible speed. These units included our Machine-Gun Battalion under Major Werner Schmidt, who had earlier served with the Berlin Police, 2nd Group, Linden Inspectorate, and then with the special Prussian police detachment within the Hermann Göring Regiment which was trained as a paratroop unit. Most of our 'Old Men' came from this unit.

Adjutant: Oberleutnant Günther Klitzing
Signals Officer: Oberleutnant Belter

1 Company: Hauptmann Otto Laun
1 Platoon: Leutnant Martin Pöppel
2 Platoon: Fahnenjunker-Feldwebel Riess
3 Platoon: Oberfeldwebel Stadlbauer

First Sergeant: Feldwebel Maul
Leader of Company HQ personnel: Feldwebel Krassa
2 Company: Oberleutnant Rieke
3 Company: Oberleutnant Leonhardt
4 Company: Hauptmann Kanthak)

Our pilot is extremely young and has no combat experience. Before this he was at school in the Reich. They've gathered aircraft from absolutely everywhere to bring the Division to the target airfield. Two years ago things were different: in those days the Division had aircraft placed specifically at its disposal and Transport Wing 30 was assigned to us. Now some of these aircraft are little more than old crates, including ours. Consequently, we're soon lagging behind the others when we finally manage to get airborne after a bad takeoff. Our pilot tries unsuccessfully to establish radio contact. We're approaching the coast, with Marseilles lying below us. On our left is Toulon, where the French Navy is based.

Ahead of us are some aircraft – they can only be our own – which are continuing on course. I lie in the nose compartment and get a fantastic view. The sea is below, an incredible deep blue, the dusk falling over it with the incomparable beauty of the south. Cumulus clouds turn orange-red, blood-red fire flowing from the setting sun. A destroyer flotilla is cutting through the water beneath us in the opposite direction to our own. The pale, speedy ships lift up out of the blue waves. Their crews wave at us as we pass overhead and we wave back, welcoming the sight of a little piece of home. We feel close to our comrades below, doing their difficult duty in these waters.

Slowly, the flock of wild birds forms up into a proper formation. At 19.00 hours Elba, where Napoleon went into exile, lies below, tiny against the massive expanse of ocean. About 50 Jus are approaching from the left, certainly from another airfield. With our greater speed, they're soon lost from sight. At 19.50 hours, we pass a powerful looking formation, then pass over Circeo. The sea is still, a beautiful blue as we pass Cap Corse, but then the darkness falls quickly. Past Naples – a thin, white column of smoke is all we can see of Vesuvius – and then at 20.30 hours we land at the nearby airfield of Capodiglino. On the perimeter are the planes which carried Düe, Geiswid, Idzykoweski and Westenberger and their teams. But where are the others? Flight control tells us that the main formation has landed at another airfield about twenty kilometres east of Naples, in

Pogliano. One of our planes is having trouble with its wheels and replacement parts are damned hard to get hold of as there are very few He-111s down here now. We take a quick decision to join the others, but are forbidden to take off because of the darkness and our lack of knowledge of local airfields and conditions. So for now we have to stay here, which won't be too bad as long as we manage to link up with the others tomorrow. Over to flight control and the phone to see what's happening over there. After some delay I get through to Feldwebel Krassa, who tells me that they've got no more information either. He'll wait for my next call at midnight.

At least we get the chance to eat a decent meal, getting our special rations, then try to get quarters at the Minerva Hotel. Success – they have clean rooms with every comfort, even – to general astonishment – a bath. The men and I feel like princes. Who knows how long it will be before we get to sleep in a bed with clean sheets again? The air-raid siren at 24.00 hours doesn't disturb the men at all, they're completely out to the wide. There's some anti-aircraft fire but it soon stops. For me personally though, it's a dreadful night. Unpleasantly warm and what's worse, having to be on the bloody telephone every hour trying to find out if anybody knows what we're meant to be doing in the morning. After all, I'm responsible for this mob and I'm just as desperate as they are to get into action. But in the end, even I manage to grab some sleep.

12 July. We're up in the early hours and travelling through Naples, though we're less impressed with it than Goethe was in his travel memoirs 'See Naples and Die'. I've found out from Krassa that the parachute equipment is being left behind. From personal experience I decide to leave the rucksacks here as well so the men haven't any unnecessary burdens to carry. The fighting won't be easy, so why should the men have to carry their baggage into it? I leave Obergefreite Loch behind with the stuff after he's volunteered for the job. Oberjäger Düe's aircraft isn't fit for take-off because of damage to the tail-wheel. 08.35 hours: we reach Pogliano after barely more than five minutes, but have to search for our unit for sometime among the mass of aircraft. Then I report to the Commander, who's delighted to have his flock together again. But we can't proceed any further due to lack of fuel. An enormous number of planes are standing on the airfield and round the perimeter. I reckon at least 300. For the first time I can also see our biggest tranport, the Giant, which has six engines and looks like a prehistoric monster. The whole thing provides an impressive display of the power of a mighty

armed empire. It's afternoon and there's still no petrol for our planes, so the prospects for take-off today are disappearing rapidly. With a lorry I've got hold of, I fetch Düe and his men and the rucksacks, which the chief has ordered me to bring after all. Then at last we're all together, roll into our blankets under the aircraft and, full of anticipation for the day ahead, finally sleep.

13 July. Today we should be away at last. As we thought, our destination is Sicily, is Catania. The date isn't too auspicious for a superstitious soldier (and we're all a little bit superstitious), but we decide that, on the contrary, it will be a good sign for us after all. Take-off is to be at 06.00 hours so there's incredible haste and activity to get ready on time. The air rumbles with the noise of hundreds of engines, the dust blots out the sun. One machine after another rolls to the cement runway and rises into the sky.

Then it's our turn. Up into the morning air, past Vesuvius and out over the open sea. Our tired old crate hasn't been able to keep up, and we're alone in the sky yet again. The pilot is getting apprehensive and would like to turn back, but I manage to keep him in harness because we'll maybe be able to link up with other aircraft during the flight. No luck so far, but we limp on. I post an observer at every window, to keep a look out for enemy fighters. The machine-guns are made ready and I clamber into the nose compartment again and pore over the map. At last we spot a small formation of Jus which we overtake, then fly along the western coast of Italy. There isn't much in the way of fortified defences to be seen, just some barbed wire entanglements here and there reaching down to the beaches. Past the Straits of Messina, and now there'll be an increasing danger of British fighters. Tension mounts, though many men still manage to fall asleep. The monotonous humming of the engines induces drowsiness and the danger of fighter attacks doesn't worry experienced men, especially when there's nothing they can do about the situation anyway. We must be very near our objective, because we can see three He-111s from our wing, recognisable by their squadron markings and numbers. All engines and maximum power so that we can get closs behind them. Christ, the pilot takes a deep breath, relieved that he's no longer alone in the sky with his little bird. Then Catania lies beneath us, the airfield comes into view and we glide in to land. 08.14 hours and we're landing on an excellent cement runway at Catania airfield.

Two of our planes are ablaze on the airfield. Has there been a raid just before we got here? If so, our tired old crate brought us luck after all. We haven't even stopped rolling when a lorry shoots out and orders us to be quick. British fighters have attacked two of our planes during landing and set them on fire, though one of the fighters was shot down. At top speed we fetch out the heavy weapons containers, throw the rucksacks into the lorry, unload the bags of supplies. A last handshake for the courageous aircrew which got us here despite all the difficulties, then off the airfield at top speed because there's a justifiable fear of fresh attacks. On the way the driver, a private in the Nazi Party Motor Corps or NSKK, tells me about the recent attack. Not far from the airfield I meet up with the chief, who orders me to move some 8 kilometres further south where the Battalion is assembling. The road is relatively good, though extremely dusty. With our vehicles jam-packed with men and equipment, we can only move slowly. We pass a sentry on the road, then we soon see our Commander Major Schmidt. Short instructions and directions to the bivouac area, and we're there.

A couple of farmsteads are scattered around here, olive groves cast their shadows, and from the little hills you can see far across the flat countryside. All in all, an idyllic place for a little rest. Allocate the sites quickly, then the men can get out of the vehicles and unload. We have to be as quick as possible, because their expecting the fighters here as well.

A little hut becomes a makeshift HQ. Under the broiling sun, the men are lugging the weapons containers under the trees and camouflaging them. I take a few minutes to give myself a wonderful cleansing wash under the nearby spring and to shave off my beard. More vehicles from 1 and 4 Companies are arriving.

In the sky we can see the first formation of four-engined enemy aircraft heading towards the airfield. Hope to God that the blokes over there see them in time and get under cover. Then the shock-waves from the explosions reach us. Columns of smoke rise and spread out till they look like thick clouds, and our thoughts are with our comrades who recently landed at the airfield. Soon Hauptmann Laun arrives with the others. Now for an assessment of our first casualties by going through the complement of each aircraft. Obergefreit Glomb killed, Unterarzt Busse with severe burns, Zartner, Wölper and Geisweis seriously wounded. In addition, two aircraft are still missing. Appalling casualties before the bloody operation has even begun, and all because they sent the formation off without any fighter escort. What kind of people have we become?

There are no new orders yet. Everyone's encamped under the olive trees, cleaning weapons and equipment, doing a fry-up or just basking in the sun. The whole farmstead is now excellently camouflaged, with no indication of any military presence.

Night comes slowly into the valley, our first night on Sicily, and a beautiful one. The moon shines brightly in the olive trees and makes us dream. Dreaming of love at home, and the happy hours we spent there. Our first night, and how many more will we watch through? How many sacrifices and how much anxiety, how much blood will be spilled here? It's quite simple – all we want is a first-class operation with an attack, like in the old days and with all the trimmings. I take my boots off and pull on my shoes, determined that tonight at least I'm going to get a reasonably comfortable sleep. Our guns are lying at hand, uniform complete, maybe this very night we'll be sent to the front line. Our Commander is receiving his orders now and, as usual, will be the last man to be able to think of sleep. The sentries have been posted on elevated ground. I dream and doze the time away.

At 22.00 hours aircraft suddenly appear overhead and our own sentries are shouting 'German paratroopers!' We know that reinforcements should be landing or making a drop some time. But shit! shit! – when the signal flares light up the errie darkness – we can see yellow and red parachutes. In an instant we all realise what's going on! British airborne troops overhead!

Still wearing my shoes, no time for anything else, sub-machine gun in my hand! Everything happening in a matter of seconds. The first prisoners are already being brought it. Great volleys of fire, a fantastic performance from our men behind their guns. More and more aircraft are arriving, gliders coasting down to earth. Our fellows behind the machine-guns are shooting like supermen. Four big American transport planes, Douglas type, crash to the ground in flames, and three gliders are set on fire. Wounded men, mostly Tommies, are brought in. The fields are full of burning straw, lighting and battlfield, and cones of machine gun fire cut through the darkness with their trajectory. Here and there I can hear the deep voices of British NCOs. Krassa gets a shot thorugh his left lower leg, has it bandaged, then starts fighting again. Other men come in with serious wounds but still want to get out there again. These are absolutely fantastic men. Prisoners are arriving constantly.

In the absence of the Commander, Hauptmann Laun has taken command of the Battalion and I'm in charge of 1 Company in his place. By morning the situation is clear and a defensive line has been established. I talk to lots of Tommies, mostly men of my own age. They're certainly not eager to fight, and their equipment looks fairly pathetic. The uniform resembles our motor vehicles combinations, though the camouflaging of the steel helmet looks useful, and their footwear is generally old and worn out. The guns look pathetic, reminding us of Russian weapons. Simply knocked together, the muzzle sight consisting of just an emergency sighting bar. Their parachute rations aren't what we remember from Crete either, and in no way comparable with our own. The only things we savour are the wonderful chocolate and – of course – the cigarettes. They're well in advance of us in one area, though, and that's the fact that they all have their own sanitary and medical equipment with them. Each man has three 1cc ampoules of morphine, water disinfectant, Atebrin and even anti-mosquito ointment. A fantastic pack, and small and handy to boot. Physically these are medium-sized, good-looking fellows, some of whom have already fought in Africa while others are direct from Britain. In my opinion their spirit is none too good. They tend to surrender as soon as they face the slightest resistance, in a way that none of our men would have done. They reckon that Mr Churchill is a good man, but not a model or example to follow. And they're not as sure of victory as they were on Crete in 1941. Their whole weaponry, ammunition and machines, comes mainly from America, and their rations from the States of that nation. All in all I get the impression that these troops are somewhat different to the ones we faced in 1941. They have deteriorated in every respect.

14 July. By morning the situation is clear. In front of us and in the west there are only straggling enemy units holding out, whilst in the east they have taken up position by the slopes and the coast road. At 05.00 hours 3 and 4 Companies each send a recce patrol into the countryside ahead to discover whether the next two thousand metres are clear of the enemy. Meanwhile we provide cover with our heavy machine-guns. Huge numbers of weapons, along with twelve prisoners, are brought in. Another recce patrol of mine under Feldwebel Jetter brings back two prisoners and a quantity of automatic weapons. At midday, 4 Company captures a number of armoured scout cars and anti-tank guns, along with seven prisoners. All the ammunition lying around nearby is blown up and the matériel and gliders destroyed. A Douglas and its attached glider are shot down by Obergefreite Dörner.

At 15.00 hours the enemy naval artillery sends some broadsides overhead, so we take refuge in a grotto and wait for it to end. Unfortunately we suffer casualties this time – Oberjäger Fischbeck and lively little Bader are both killed and Jetter receives a slight head wound. It's a bloody mess. Those dogs out there in their tubs can fire just like they're on maneouvres and we're just sitting targets. Meanwhile, 2 and 3 Companies have taken control of the hill but been driven back to their old positions by the ceaseless fire of the naval artillery. Casualties on both sides.

At 18.00 hours two enemy armoured scout cars drive up close to Battalion HQ. The first shot misses by ten metres, then Oberleutnant Tiesen tries to engage them in close combat and is killed. After a short time, thank God, they turn away to the south. However, as things now stand, if the Battalion stays in this area for any length of time it will be completely trapped by British forces advancing from the south.

Since our Commander is currently discussing the situation with the General, at 19.30 hours Hauptmann Laun gives the order to withdraw to 'Simeto' Hill, that's the little river that we crossed on the journey here. It's already getting dark as the first units of the Battalion begin to assemble near us in a little olive grove. Oberleutnant Rieke provides rear cover in a masterly fashion whilst I concentrate on securing the flank. The most humiliating thing for our Company is the fact that we've got no means of transport and so, apart from our weapons and ammunition, can only take the bare essentials with us. Our rucksacks and all our spare clothing have to be left behind, so we pile them up and set them alight. I was right in Naples when I suggested that everything superfluous should be left behind, but there's nothing to be done now. I sit in the trench and watch the arrival of the various Companies. Just pray things go well. All it needs is for some well-directed mortar fire into the middle of us – but fortunately it doesn't happen. The enemy has certainly been made extremely cautious by the destruction of his airborne forces and is bound to pursue us very slowly and cautiously from now on.

Some of the prisoners, around a hundred, are sent back first. Then the Battalion sets off in a long column with 4 Company at its head. To avoid being recognised by advancing enemy units, Haumptmann Laun resorts to a trick. He makes us take off our helments and gets the Tommies marching between us to keep theirs on. It seems to work. However, this struggle with our gear, the equipment and guns, the need to drag weapons containers on their tiny wheels, it may be using up the last reserves of our strength. As soon as there's a break the men collapse into an exhausted sleep. But the journey still isn't over. We march past a shattered fighter airfield and then reach an anti-aircraft position where we're to make our defence. The food's still cooking – that's how quickly its former defenders have shoved off – but we've no desire to eat just now. Instead, we drop into the hay for one and a half hours of wonderful sleep. The Tommies grant my request not to disturb us – they'll be too tired themselves. Slowly it's grown quiet. Apart from the sentries, everyone is asleep.

What's going to happen next? The fact that we've made a tactical retreat here isn't too serious, but the way these anti-aircraft positions have been abandoned doesn't speak much for the fighting spirit of the German troops who were here before. They've been allowed to get soft, living in the land of the citrus groves.

15 July. Awake again at 06.00 hours, then select and occupy defensive positions. The numerous bomb craters offer adequate defence against artillery fire, so the most important thing at the moment is camouflage. A recce patrol under Feldwebel Riess brings two prisoners back. Some British airborne troops have also landed here – obviously put down in the wrong place. The day passes quietly, despite the moderate artillery fire.

At 20.00 hours five enemy heavy cruisers and a large number of destroyers sail past quite unmolested, heading northwards and very near to the coast. It's an impressive display of force, bound to cheer the Tommies but depressing and humiliating for us. We work throughout the night to construct our defensive positions. More than anything else we've got to provide some protection against the burning sun, and to stop enemy aircraft spotting us.

16 July. Punctually at 01.00 hours artillery fire begins along our left sector. It's quickly followed by a British attack, which is beaten back. Where we are there's only light harassing fire, otherwise things stay quiet. Then at 20.00 hours there's renewed artillery fire on our left, and tank movements. So far we haven't received any precise situation reports.

17 July. Morning passes with light shooting – aimed more at the anti-aircraft battery to our rear – otherwise quiet. But physically I feel sick as a dog, aching limbs, headache, dry throat, the whole works. Stragglers, infantrymen, make their way in. They're from a fortress construction battalion from Lake Constance and were forced to retreat here earlier today by enemy tanks. On our left we now have a hole 2.5 kilometres wide and no reserve troops. These infantrymen,

mostly older men, seem thoroughly weary and lacking in fighting spirit. Towards evening the Commander decides on a withdrawal. The next line is to be held about 500 metres north of here. We move out without being spotted.

By now I'm so ill that I can't even walk by myself. Oberjäger Wolff helps me, but we can't keep up with the pace. Suddenly we're alone, don't know the way and find ourselves just wandering about. Eventually we hear the sound of spades being used, so we must have managed to find the right place purely by chance. Then we come across Oberleutnant Rieke who gives us more directions. After we find a little gatekeeper's house I collapse, too weak to go any further. I send Wolff to the Hauptmann and fall asleep.

18 July. At 08.00 hours I suddenly hear noises outside. Pistol in hand, I creep outside like 'Old Shatterhand' himself. But it's only a mortar section moving into position here. I take my leave, finally approach a red house and report to the Commander. The Company has taken up position in an old anti-aircraft gun emplacement hastily abandoned by its crew. It's a miserable sight, everything lying around. Stores with clothing and equipment, a complete orderly room with secret division orders lying open and in full view, also tailor's equipment and a superb shoemaker's workshop. They were carrying on a real peacetime lifestyle here, but it was irresponsible to leave everything lying around when they retreated.

At 10.00 hours the enemy artillery chucks a few shells in our direction. It's not surprising, since the men have begun to behave as if it's peacetime, fetching water from nearby streams although the countryside here is fully visible to men in the hills opposite.

Afterwards I make my way to the aid station, take my leave of the Commander and a few hours later I'm travelling in an Italian armoured car to the military hospital in Catania. This is a superb hospital, built high up on a hill, with large airy terraces. When I arrive, I suspect that the Sicilian campaign is already over as far as I'm concerned, but in fact the good food soon brings me back to health. There are a lot of wounded men being moved out at the moment, mainly Tommies being taken to Messina.

At first I find myself sharing a room with three ordinary soldiers. Thank God, it's got a mosquito net as well. The whole place is incredible, and if I wasn't so damned sick I'd be happy just to sit in one of the deck-chairs on the sunny terrace. First and foremost though, I must get out of these clothes. My whole body is covered with flea bites, with a thousand tiny holes. I suppose we all look the same.

There's an air-raid warning at around midnight. They have to carry me out, otherwise I'd never have got up at all. However, the planes fly past and this calms things down, since Catania looks as if it has already had a bad time.

19 July. Nobody here is taking care of us, there's only a few weary medical orderlies sprawling around in the corridors. Eventually one of them arrives and brings coffee, at least. Then, in response to my own energetic requests, they fetch us biscuits and cheese. In the Bay of Catania two light cruisers are bombarding the south-west quarter of the town. At 11.00 hours I'm moved to a comfortable officer's room, with an excellent feather bed, decent wardrobes and, most important of all, a bathroom next door. It would be nice to stay here a while, but I'm already so much better as a result of the proper diet that I'm hoping to be on my way again tomorrow. In the evening I spend a few hours with the doctor in charge here, Major Klingelböfer, and Dr Ruth, whom I already know from the Battalion. For the first time I get to hear more news of the war, especially about the bitter fighting in the east.

20 July. I'm dressed and ready, waiting only for transport. Eventually I manage to cadge a lift to the aid station, confident that I can make my way back from there. By the time I reach the Battalion with a medical orderly, it's 22.00 hours. Good to see that they're glad to have me back safe and well. Then it's time for explanations as the Commander describes the Company's latest triumphs. He says that this morning, after a bombardment of four hours, the Company beat back an English attack without suffering any casualties itself. The enemy attack was supported by ten tanks and supporting fire. But our men fought like the devil and knocked out five of them, whilst another two had already been destroyed by the 8.8cm anti-aircraft fire. The *pièce de résistance* came from Feldwebel Schach, who set two tanks on fire with an anti-tank mine. It was a bad day for the Tommies, who suffered a lot of casualties whilst we didn't have any. A few days later, this triumph was also reported in the communiqué of the High Command. However, it turned out that one man from the signal communication platoon was shot dead in the road ditch by one of the British tank commanders.

Our conversation is suddenly interrupted by an abrupt resumption of artillery fire – again in the sector defended by my own Company and 2 Company. The stikes are too numerous to count, but there are at least four per second. How have the British managed to move in such a massive quantity of artillery? No answer from our

Die Landungen auf Sizi

vom 10.-15. Juli 1943

Maßstab ungef. 1:2000000

N

Ustica

PALERMO

TRAPANI

Cefalu

Termini Jmerese

22.7.

23.7.

1975

Marsala

28/ Assietta
23.7.

it.XII
A.K.
683

Corleone

Lercara Friddi

Castelvetrano

15.P.G.D.

28/ Aosta

12./13. 7.

S.Cataldo Livorno

Caltan

Sciacca

Pistani

2.Panz.Div.

Canicatti
3.Div.

Agrigento

Porto Empedocle
16.7.

4.S.Div.
12.7.

Licata

Zeichenerklärung

Deutsch-ital. Divisionen

Deutsche Bewegungen

Simeto-Dittaino-Stellung ab 16.7.

Ätna-Stellung ab 1.8.

Luftlandungen

Brit. 8. Armee

US. 7. Armee

Flugplätze

3.Div.

Ranger

2.Pz.Div.

schwimm.Reserve

II. Korps

US. 7. Armee
10.Juli

Catanzaro

Gioiatauro
Palmi
Bagnara Cal.

Milazzo   15.7.
Locri

MESSINA   ab 15.7.   29. P.G.D.

REGGIO
CALABRIA

Randazzo   H.G.
bis 10.7.

Troina   Bronte Ätna   Taormina

Adrano   14.7.

Centuripe   Paterno   Acireale

Misterbianco

CATANIA
12./13.7.

Brit. 1. Fj. Brig.
13.7.

13.7. – 3. Commando   Brit. 1. LL. Brig.
(Anflug v. Süden)

Agnone

Lentini   Carlentini   Gruppe Schmalz

Francofonte   Augusta

Sortino

Vizzini   Melilli

Syrakus   Commando

Brit.

Ragusa   Noto

S. Div.   XIII. Korps

50. Div.

Rosolini
Ispica

Pachino   C. Passero   231. Inf. Brig.   10. Juli
Britische 8. Armee

Kanad. 1. Div.   51. Div.

XXX. Korps

129

side. The earth trembles and shakes so much that it seems like the end of the world. What's more, it carries on a bloody long time. Telephone connections were cut some time ago, and the wind carries the clouds of powder over to us. After an hour and a half – though to us it seems an eternity – it finally stops. When the telephone's working again a few hours later, Haumptmann Laun reports that the artillery fire has been withstood without any casualties, and that our weapons are all intact. Comforted, we're all soon asleep.

21 July. At 09.00 hours a messenger fetches me back to the Company command post. The chief is pleased to have his platoon leader back, and I'm even more delighted to be back with my mob. Everyone's still here – except for my oldest Obergefreite, Ralpe, killed by an accidental hit which also wounded Oberjäger Düe. It's a serious loss for us all. This morning, as the chief tells me, the Company's had another triumph. The Tommies obviously thought that their artillery fire yesterday had made us withdraw, and arrived early this morning with three lorries packed full of infantrymen. Hitched up behind were 3.7 and 5.7 antitank guns. Clearly they didn't understand our paratroopers and had learned nothing from their experiences yesterday. Everything was quiet. My boys let the motor cycle escort past and only let them have it when the lorries were right next to them. Within a matter of seconds the first truck was in flames, with Tommies jumping out as best they could. At the end of it we counted fifteen dead and brought back eleven prisoners. Only a few of them managed to escape into the vineyards. In the evening we fetch the antitank guns back – they'll strengthen our defences considerably. The rest of the day passes quietly, despite moderate artillery fire from the Tommies.

22 July. Nothing new happens overnight. Early in the morning a recce patrol under Feldwebel Krassa sets out and discovers that the Tommies have moved away to the west.

The sun's heat and glare is scorching down on us, so I finally decide to move the company command post to the red house. First of all we have to move the dead horse that's lying in front of it – the thing stinks to high heaven. Life is more pleasant here. The camp beds we find there do good service: put a mosquito net over them and there you are – like Uncle Tom's Cabin. In addition, we've set up a lending library which helps the men cope with the inevitable moments of boredom. We're also managing to get letters sent out again.

23 July. All quiet again, apart from a certain amount of harassing fire. The enemy artillery seems to have been reduced a certain amount here to reinforce the point of main effort in the west. We don't object to that. As for the infantry, well, they know all about us by now.

24 July. Now for a number of quiet days, because our position is so good that the enemy is scarcely likely to try anything during the daytime. Along with Sulima and the Kischuss gun crew, I set off to the rear, into even more peaceful countryside. About 2 kilometres to the north we come across a large vineyard with a stream running through it, which is just what we want. There's been an anti-aircraft gun here too, you can tell by the equipment and clothing left lying about. It's a miserable spectacle, so much equipment abandoned, equipment that our womenfolk at home worked so hard to manufacture. However, we set to work with a will, Sicilian women glad to help us in return for some bars of soap. The men look funny in their underpants, behaving as if there were no women there at all. But as we haven't anything else, our trousers are wet and the women don't seem to mind, nobody bothers. The owner invites me in for a glass of red wine, which tastes marvellous. The other people there have disappeared into the cellar out of fear; maybe they're afraid that their heads will get blown off up above. But it's actually wonderfully peaceful here – only a few shells thunder overhead now and then, and they are aimed at the artillery behind us.

When we return at 21.00 hours we're greeted by bad news from our position. One man has been killed and four badly wounded by a direct hit from a mortar shell. As ever, it's the best men in the Company. Ossaschnik is dead, Scholz, Vosch, Frick and a man from 3 Platoon seriously hurt. A bad blow for our Company, particularly since the best of our mortar teams were involved. When I report to the chief, he's also badly affected by our losses.

25 July. All quiet except for the artillery fire, which now lasts the whole morning.

26 July. All quiet today as well. But this bloody harassing fire wounds another of our men, Obergefreite Krener. However, there's good news for our Company and for my old comrade in arms Eugen Scherer, who is promoted to Leutnant today. I had quietly handed in my other epaulettes at Battalion. Great rejoicing in the Company at this reward, which is thoroughly deserved.

27 July. Two more men were wounded today by direct artillery hits, Oberjäger Manthey and Obergefreite Schmidt. Along the

entire sector, but particularly around our command post, the harassing fire is more intense than before. The heat remains almost unendurable, thousands of flies buzzing around us so that the chief and I have to arm ourselves with towels the whole time to drive the wretched things away. When the men come in for their rations in the evening they're totally incapable of being spoken to for half an hour. We call this cussedness 'Chirocco' after the unnerving south wind.

28 July. Relatively quiet until evening. At 20.22 hours sudden artillery fire, coupled with heavy mortar fire and heavy machine-gun fire in 2 Company's sector. Despite the ceaseless bombardment the heavy machine-gun fire is returned by our own heavy machine guns and mortars. Then at 22.00 hours we're relieved by Leonhardt's Company. The positions are changed group by group. I'd already been over there this morning with my group leaders, so that the relief operation went smoothly. Today our Commander, Haptmann Laun, finally has to take leave of us. His old illness is flaring up again to such an extent that the consequences would be serious if he stayed any longer. He bids us farewell with a heavy heart, and we're equally sad to see him go. Before he leaves he gives me a Company order to read tomorrow. Now I'm to lead the Company in this fighting. I'm honoured to be given this responsibility, and just hoping that things go well.

29 July. The day is spent extending our defensive positions. I have the Company command post set up in the 'White House'. It's got strong walls and a superb view of the positions occupied by the entire Battalion. I don't understand why a Forward Observation Officer hasn't been put here. With Feldwebel Riess I get in touch with Oberleutnant Dittmar, my neighbour on the right. In the afternoon we make a limited raid into the hinterland and find all sorts of useful equipment in the abandoned anti-aircraft gun emplacements.

30 July. No undue happenings today. Absolutely no sign of Tommy at all. In the evening 3 Company, in our old position, comes under heavy fire. Now we can see for the first time the sort of fire we were under during our time there. Shell after shell, landing so close together it's impossible to count them. You'd think there'd be nothing left alive there at all. The smoke blots out all light. When the haze clears we can see that our old command post, the 'Red House', has also been hit. All we can do is hope that Oberleutnant Leonhardt has survived. When the telephone connections are restored, there's great relief as we discover that despite the heavy bombardment Leonhardt and his men have suffered no casualties at all.

30 July. Company commanders' meeting at 15.00 hours. To our astonishment the Commander tells us that we're to withdraw still further. The leadership is abandoning Sicily. The decision is completely incomprehensible to us all and comes as a real hammer blow. On the mainland there are whole Divisions which could come across, entire tank regiments are waiting to be transported. The situation is far from disastrous – Tommy's scared and we're more eager to attack than ever. It looks as though the retreat is solely due to political conditions in Italy. Militarily we could be strong enough to drive the Tommies and the Yanks from the island. For soldiers who are used only to attacking and then to standing firm in defensive positions, such a retreat, such an abandonment of a whole country, is devastating. But when we discover that Mussolini has 'abdicated' or stepped down, the mystery becomes more comprehensible. Apparently our partner in the Axis has had enough. Like many of the others, I'm shocked to hear of Mussolini's fall: after all, he's a friend of the Führer and I regard him an upright character. On the other hand, when you look at the classes ranged against him, the Church, the Royal Family, the senior officer corps who have rallied to Badoglio, then you can understand what has happened. The preparations to carry out 'Operation Simeto' are soon completed. 3 Company under Lieutnant Leonhardt is to stay in position, the remainder of 2 and 3 Companies to pull back to Line A whilst we go straight through to Line B. That's the plan. We're only waiting for the order.

1 August. Nothing else has happened. Is this to be yet another so-called 'Luftwaffe Holiday', seeing as it's Sunday? The harassing fire is slight and only intensifies towards evening. At Mass.a.Fichera the observation posts have spotted an advanced English observer working with messenger dogs. You have to hand it to Tommy, he gets his Forward Observation Officer in position bloody quickly and his artillery fires itself in very fast.

2 August. Company commanders meeting at 21.00 hours. Today's the day. The Company's routes have been changed, as the previous ones are too vulnerable to enemy fire at night. The mules that we've acquired are moved up quickly and then we move off, rapidly and silently, at around 23.00 hours. The Company leaves its positions and marches with the mules and the carts to the road to Catania. 4 Company is meant to be meeting up with us, but it only makes contact with us at the market place there.

3 August. It's already growing light as we reach Line B. Oberleutnant Dittmar, put in charge of me and my shrunken Company, fills me in on the situation and tells me about the sector. We tour the whole area until 10.00 hours, by which time the best positions have been found and are quickly occupied. From up ahead comes the comforting news that the enemy is continuing to fire on our old positions, which are occupied only by a few troops as combat outposts of Line A. then there's another damn problem. All the owners of the mules, horses and carts come to me wanting their animals back, or payment for them. The whole thing is crazy. I argue with them until there's actual shooting in Mascaluccia, which is only brought to an end when we bring up an anti-tank gun. After that there's a great deal of haggling, with Generals and Consuls arriving to mediate. Meanwhile we've set up our heavy machine-guns in the town and explained the state of siege. Next day feelings have calmed down.

4 August. All quiet where we are, but tanks have appeared in our old positions. In line with their orders, the combat outposts have withdrawn. However, Line A is in limbo as a result of the premature and cowardly retreat of the Körner Regiment and will have to be withdrawn tonight. 2 and 3 Companies will then move through to Line C.

5 August. As a result of all this we're in the front line again and have to be constantly on the alert. There's plenty of ammunition in the positions here so we've no anxiety on that score. At midday the sentries report bells ringing and cheering in Misterbianca, then the noise of engines. A recce patrol, sent out to establish contact with the units on our left, also reports enemy units in front of Gustmann's position. Krassa has been in Barriera, where the civilians had attempted to deal with some mines and eight people had been killed.

Two armoured scout cars travelling in our direction turn back towards Barriera. I send Obergefreite Schmiessing with Deves and Knies to Canniena as a stationary bicycle patrol. Up to 19.00 hours they have nothing significant to report, but return at 19.30 hours to report that the enemy, about a company strong, is moving towards M. Now things are getting more interesting, since B is only about 400 metres from my position. At 20.00 hours there's heavy machine gun fire from the south-west aimed at Idzykowski's position. Krassa comes back with some horror stories and reports which understandably make the Commander's hackles rise, so much so that he himself comes forward along with a messenger and me to the

Idzykowski gun. But in fact, though the gun mount has been hit by the extremely accurate enemy fire and is out of action, by some miracle nobody has been hurt. The rest of the night is quiet. Only the occasional signal flare from Tommy, who's obviously shit scared.

6 August. Another day's hard fighting for us, beginning in the early hours. British recce patrols inch carefully forward, sounding out the area. We let them come as far as possible and then hit them hard.

At 07.00 hours we can hear the sound of hand grenades and machine-gun fire from the unit on our left – that is, from Gustmann's men (he was also my neighbour during the winter campaign in Russia on the Szappszo Lake). At 07.40 hours Sulima reports that he has fired on a recce patrol consisting of four Tommies and that one has been left lying wounded. Schmiesing also hits a Tommy somewhat later at the edge of Giovanni di Gerlermo, forcing the others to retreat. Since 08.00 hours there have been reports of increased enemy activity on the eastern edge of Giovanni.

At 10.30 hours we get some fantastic action. A messenger from the advanced anti-tank gun comes running in to report: 'Tommies on our left!' Things could well get lively, it's only seventy metres away. Everyone grabs their gun and heads for the anti-tank position at breakneck speed. We jump down the stone wall towards them – between four and six metres high – and we're there, falling on them like the devil. There's some fierce close combat before we drive them off and get time for a well-earned cigarette. But they almost caught us in our combat post in this broken countryside, damn it. Amazing to see Krassa arrive, grab a light mortar from a wounded Tommy and keep on shooting. The boys were all superb, all joining in, none hesitated or stayed out of the way. And we got good results too, even though a lot of the Tommies managed to get away. We brought back six prisoners, found several corpses and spotted trials of blood leading back towards the enemy lines. We had no casualties ourselves, proving that when you go in hard and courageously you get the best results. Everyone is inspired by this success, and nobody pays any more thought to the fact that the Tommies had come very close to wiping us all out.

Earlier in the day Schröder had observed more enemy troops and fired on them, whilst Idzykrowski also had a magnificent success. He was just about to light a cigarette when a scouting party appeared in front of him. In one movement he raised his sub-machine gun and fired. The result was two men killed, including a Second Lieutenant, and four wounded Tommies brought in. Valuable maps found as well. Further observation shows that the enemy has established a base in a house about 400 metres in front of us. Krassa goes forward with a patrol, gets the light mortar we've seized into position and takes aim at the house. Unfortunately after only a few shots a shell explodes in a tree, showering its shrapnel downwards and wounding Krassa severely in the right arm. Druba is also wounded, though only slightly. Both men carry on firing. Feldwebel Riess gets back with a prisoner and reports to me that the blood trails he's found indicate that the enemy has suffered more casualties. Our right flank is also keeping busy: approximately 50-60 Tommies moving down through the ravine from north to south. Jetter lets them get good and close and then lets them have it, shooting down at least 40 of them for sure. At 18.45 hours Schmiesing reports new successes. At the eastern exit of Giovanni he shoots down three out of a party of 15 men, and another four are carried away by the retreating Tommies. Horn is doing his part, providing a hail of accurate fire from the gun with telescopic sight. So the day comes to an end, a day filled with heavy casualties for the British, whilst we celebrate our successes with some of those excellent English cigarettes. At 21.00 hours another enemy patrol is driven back. Shortly afterwards we receive the order to 'walk' at 22.00 hours. Signal flares light the sky here and there – a very restless night. My messengers scoot through the section with the relief orders, whilst our armoured car drives away guns, equipment and ammunition. Weber harnesses the mules and parks the carts by the side of the road. At 22.20 hours on the dot the entire Company moves silently from its positions and gathers at the Company command post, except for Jetter's gun crew which is to join us later. Sulima stays behind as rear guard until the Company reaches Gravina. By 22.00 hours the Company has left Scalagranda down to the last man and taken up position in Gravina de Catania. But our gipsy wanderings continue, through Tremestrieri – S.Giovanni – di Punta-Viagrande to Barriera, where we're to act initially as Battalion reserve.

4 Company arrives at Line C at the same time. There are engineers everywhere, mining roads, preparing bridges for demolition and installing all kinds of 'joke' articles. But it's certain that Tommy won't be laughing himself to death over them. By the time we reach the assembly area it's 03.00 hours. Since it's still dark and the men have to be accommodated, we decide to open up the houses. In the first one all hell is let loose with women screaming,

men rushing around thinking that they're being attacked. But when we show them that we're not Tommies, everything is fine. We find quarters and the men fall into an exhausted sleep after their long, difficult day. I also collapse into a chair and fall asleep at once. But in my case it's no use, since in an hour's time I have to report to the Commander.

7 August. Dog-tired, I travel in our Lancia to the Commander in Penise, where I discover that I could easily have arrived later (damn it!). For tactical purposes we are placed under the command of 4 Company, but for the time being we're to remain in Battalion reserve in Barriera. Back to the mob, where at least I get time to look round the camp site whilst the boys are still asleep. There's heavy enemy artillery fire aimed at the rear guards some five kilometres ahead of us. Just in front of us there are some enormous super-heavy guns in firing position. Now it's not exactly a pleasant feeling to have this enormous volcano-thing right in front of your nose. In fact, it's almost worse for us than for the Tommies when the enormous debris from its rocket-propelled shells comes thundering through the air. It's a vast thing with six barrels, but so light that six men can pull it. Further forward there's an 8.8 battery which is also firing at the Tommies.

8 August. The rest is absolutely fantastic. I'm lying in a comfortable deck-chair, dreaming and sunning myself and really doing myself some good. At midday there's heavy enemy artillery fire directed at the artillery positions ahead of us.

Even where we are, the dust drives us down into the wine cellar. The shells are also being directed at the Barriera-Piataforte junction, a route along which all our retreating forces will have to pass. Now, after the departure of more sick men, the whole Company consists of only 23 men – scarcely more than a platoon at war strength.

At 21.15 hours the warning order comes for a *kleinen Reise*. Since we're under fire already, that won't be so easy. All I can do is hope that we stay lucky.

At 24.00 hours we set off in groups. Shortly before that there's an even heavier concentration of artillery fire on the road we'll be moving down. So, the most important thing is to keep a good distance between the men. I send the armoured car on ahead as far as Fleri where it will be safe, and just keep my ammunition and weapons wagon here. There's more artillery fire on the road, about 200 metres ahead of us. As I go on slightly ahead of the Company with my car, we hear the cry: 'Comrades, there are three severely

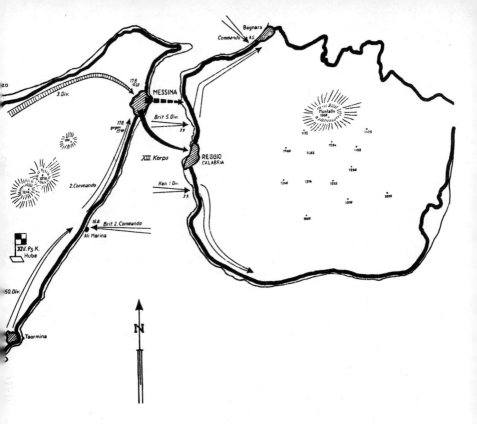

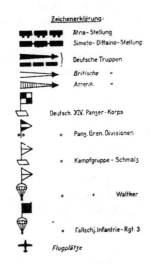

Die Schlacht um den ÄTNA

Maßstab ungef. 1:400 000

Zeichenerklärung:

	Ätna-Stellung
	Simeto-Dittaino-Stellung
	Deutsche Truppen
	Britische "
	Amerik. "
	Deutsch. XIV. Panzer-Korps
	" Panz. Gren. Divisionen
	" Kampfgruppe - Schmalz
	" " Walther
	" Fallschj. Infantrie-Rgt. 3
	Flugplätze

wounded paratroopers here!' We stop immediately and I'm deeply shaken to see that Oberleutnant Leonhardt, the Commander of 3 Company, is among them. His pulse is still there but very faint – enough to make you weep. We lift him carefully into the car and travel on, hoping that perhaps he can still be saved. But by the time we meet up with Oberarzt Dr Pazelt and the ambulance on the way, this fine officer, who has been with us since Crete, is dead. When I report this to the Commander, he is deeply distressed. For all of us, it's a terrible loss, almost incomprehensible. All the same, we don't feel any hatred for the Tommies, only for that cowardly pack, the Italians. The fact that we've got to hold out on behalf of these faithless sods – it's enough to make you puke. Then three more men are brought to the clearing station with splinter wounds.

So I can get my bearings properly, I reach for my map – but it's not there. It has the entire situation and our defensive positions as far as C3 on it – a disaster if it should fall into enemy hands. And the enemy has had three hours to reach our old position and find it. But there's nothing for it, I have to go back again at whatever cost. Into the ammunition and weapons wagon and back as quickly as possible, past a burning Tiger tank, past long columns of infantry. Thank God, at the road junction we come across one of Körner's covering parties, the last. Race into the house, but the map isn't here either. Shit, but there's nothing to be done – I must have lost the thing somewhere on the way. (Later I discover that Leutnant Scherer had been to the house to get his bearings and had taken the map with him. My thoughtlessness could have cost the lives of many of my comrades.) Anyway, for three days I've been suffering from some form of amnesia, forgetting absolutely everything under the sun. By the time I get back to my mob in Bongiardo, a suburb of Santa Verenina, it's almost morning.

9 August. In the meantime, Oberleutnant Dittmar has already guided my Feldwebel Sulima into our sector of the occupied positions. By the time various adjustments have been made and the situation is clear, it's midday. Oberleutnant Gustmann – once again my neighbour on the left flank – establishes connections with me and everything is soon organised. Of the enemy, there's nothing to be seen as yet and in front of us there are the combat outposts which aren't removed until 12.00 hours. Scherer has been given a difficult job. In front of him are the hills from which Tommy can fire down – and then move back out of danger in the clear light of day, under the burning sun.

We hope that the sun has the same effect on the enemy and makes him less attentive. Then Scherer can push straight through to Line D, which runs along the Mascalia-Milo hill. At 18.30 hours we get the first sightings of the enemy. Two armoured scout cars move out of Fleri and stop by a house about 800 metres ahead of us. Soon after that there's some well-aimed artillery fire from the Tommies – yet again, they've got their Forward Observation Officer in place first. We don't suffer any casualties and it's clear that he isn't aware of our exact positions yet. Shortly after that, some British infantrymen arrive in four armoured scout cars. To us it seems a really stupid move. Our first heavy machine-gun salvoes land directly on target and make the Tommies clamber out and veer away as quickly as possible. They're forced to abandon one of their Bren gun carriers, so we send one of our own vehicles out to retrieve it. Oberleutnant Dittmar passes on the warning order for a *grossen Reise* at 05.00 hours on 10 August. So, we're to move back yet again. The whole operation is being carried out supremely well. Tommy is meeting constant resistance, is unsure of our strength, and is therefore cautious about advancing. They haven't got the guts to break straight through. When they come to a line which is good and secure – even though it may not be held by large numbers of defenders – they are brought to a halt for some time. All the same, I'm bound to admit that this broken countryside is easy to defend but difficult to attack. Even when weak forces are overrun, they still have a good chance to make it back to their own lines. Things have quietened down a bit here so at 22.00 hours I order the mule train to pull out.

10 August. Promptly at 05.00 hours we get under way, silently as ever. Jetter provides cover with two guns, Sulima takes another route through the town and guards the bridge there until we arrive. The British 5.7cm antitank gun which we captured is blown up since we can't take it with us any more. 4 Company departs, then I follow with the rest. By 05.30 hours all the men have assembled by the bridge. Sulima moves out to Dragala to the motor vehicle assembly point, whilst Jetter remains on guard until the bridge is blown up at 06.00 hours. Then we're away. However, Obergefreite Nehls, who was sent to drive a lorry to the assembly point last night, is still missing. Perhaps been taken prisoner by the Tommies – in his case, it would be no surprise since he's had more than a bellyful of this. We stop at Dragal, then continue via S.Antonio – Machia – Nunciata to the Battalion assembly point about four kilometres to the north. It's situated in olive and lemon groves and is wonderfully peaceful. For

the time being the Battalion – currently consisting only of ourselves, 4 Company and the Staff – is to stay here as battle group reserve. And if we're really lucky, then in a few days we'll be relieved and ferried across to the mainland. It's scarcely credible but is nevertheless possible, since my right flank is very close to Etna. By this shortening of the line, more units could be taken out of action and deployed elsewhere. Line E is running through here now. Where will the alphabet end?

11 August. We're on the lookout for abandoned vehicles, at first without success. But as I've absolutely no desire to travel on foot or by mule, I'm determined to organise some transport. When we get back I find out that there's a Company Commanders' discussion set for 14.30 hours. Meanwhile 2 and 3 Companies have come back from C3. Tonight we're to transfer together with 2 Company some forty kilometres northwards, that is, still further from the front. Perhaps we'll soon be crossing to the mainland. This whole business surely can't last much longer. We move off at dusk.

We have to get past some stretches of the route quickly since they are visible to the enemy and frequently come under fire from the enemy artillery and naval artillery. In the morning Oscar gets hold of another enormous lorry – Italian, a four-ton ambulance. So, squashed together somewhat, we travel through Piedimonte – Fiumefreddo – Giardini – S.Allasio to Roccalumero, and then westwards into the hills to Pagliara. We arrive at 23.00 hours and find quarters.

12 August. At first light we're moving again, to Messina to organise vehicles, a lorry full of drivers. The situation in Messina is such that five ferries are available for the German units and just one for the Italians. In consequence, the Italians are leaving much of their equipment behind on the quay. However, this gives us a last, wonderful opportunity to obtain some transport. The town is in ruins. Tram and telephone cables are lying in the road, and although we can see many civilians moving around, it's clear that the place itself is dead. Columns of Italian infantry move past, including paratroop units. They look bizarre, our Axis colleagues. We still haven't heard – at least not here in Sicily – of any heroic deeds on their part. I soon manage to find some abandoned vehicles on the main street, still loaded with really valuable equipment which will all be lost. In barely four hours we make five lorries serviceable, and a nippy little motor-bike for me. The Battalion will be delighted, since we came over without any vehicles. We've managed to organise

our own, but then this is an ability which we're already famous for. Now my men are busy washing and shaking off the dust of Sicily.

Tomorrow we'll be crossing back to the mainland. The Commander arrives with the others and orders are given out for the next day. These state that we're to be taken across at 05.00 hours and is good news as far as we're concerned – we'll be glad to see the back of the place. It's a good thing that it's so light since it gives us plenty of time to get ready.

13 August. Our day of destiny? We came over here on the thirteenth day of one month, and are going back on the thirteenth day of another. Only four weeks here, but they have been incredibly eventful. We came across determined to win, to defeat the enemy completely, but what happened? We aren't the hunters, but the hunted. Our only consolation is that we've been forced to evacuate the island because of orders from above, and not out of weakness. We might almost be satisfied, except that we have left our comrades lying here, left them behind in enemy territory.

But we're not back on the mainland yet. First of all we have to reach Messina without being wiped out by the naval artillery, then we've got to avoid being bombed in Messina itself, and finally we've got to make the crossing safely. After long delays, we arrive in Messina at 07.00 hours, make our way slowly to the ferry and then wait.

An Italian assault division – fully motorised – crosses ahead of us. They arrived with full equipment and are being allowed to take all of it across on a German ferry. Their men look incredibly spruce and smart and can't have seen much action. This 'assault division' clearly hasn't done much attacking, despite its name.

Air raid warning at 10.00 hours. A few bombs fall into the water, then it's over. Enemy aircraft can't do much here, since over on the mainland they face the strongest active air defence system of the war to date.

At last, at 15.00 hours we're on our way. The ferry takes 2 Company and ourselves with four lorries and two motorcycles. Slowly, it moves away from Sicily. Our thoughts go beyond Messina to the paratroop position, to Simeto where things were so hot for us and where we lost brave comrades. We did our duty and perhaps rather more than that, and it certainly isn't our fault that we are being forced to retreat. It has only taken the Tommies and the Yanks a few weeks to conquer this advance bastion of Europe, so they can use it as a springboard to the Continent. But our dead did their duty and our struggle wasn't in vain, even here. The superb disengagement won more time for the leadership.

We needed this time for the organisation of a proper defence against an invasion attempt. All of us hope that, after the conclusion of the Sicilian campaign, German units will be withdrawn from southern Italy. Why should we stay? We can't be of service to Germany here, the Italians will cut and run like they did before. So it would be better to create a strong front further up. That's the only thing that will protect us.

Hardly anyone thinks of home. Oh, it would be wonderful to be there, but we're soldiers, the Führer's best troops, and there's no such thing as leave in times as turbulent as these. We need just a little time to recover, then we'll be ready for action again. In my old Company command post I left a message behind for Tommy, expressing the hope that we'd soon meet again, on another battlefield.

During the crossing there's another air raid warning, but the 2cm shipboard anti-aircraft artillery soon drives the Spitfires away. In half-an-hour or so we're on the Italian mainland.

Directed by Leutnant Goldmann, we take the mountain road to Gallico. Damned narrow mountain paths, as if they've been built for defence. There are antitank obstacles, but made of such flimsy material that they start to crumble as soon as a lorry goes past. Through Gallico – Marina – Lagandi – Allessio to San Stefano. On this high plateau there are Italian commandos everywhere, and obstacles to provide defence against gliders. Everything seems prepared for a defensive operation. But it was the same in Sicily, yet despite their strong defensive positions the Italians turned and ran at the least sign of resistance.

We lose our bearings a few times but eventually reach our assembly point via Delianuova – Giorgia – Lubrichi – Calabretto and bivouac for the night (it's already dark by this time). The battle for Sicily is over, the Sicilian chapter concluded.

What will become of us in Italy?

10 July 1943. The Allied invasion of Sicily has begun. The Machine Gun Battalion is transported to Naples from Airfield Orange in southern France, mainly in He 111 aircraft. Ultimate destination: Catania.

Loading the aerial delivery containers.

At 18.00 hours on 12 July 1943, 3 Parachute Regiment made its drop south of Catania airfield without casualties. The Engineer Battalion and units of 4 Parachute Regiment followed next day.

An English breakthrough is halted. At the most advanced German positions, ground cloths are laid out to show the Luftwaffe the main line of battle.

posite page): Paratroopers landing
h west of Catania. Despite enemy
'ing and artillery bombardment,
advance successfully.

A US bomber crashes just in front of the German lines, brought down by 8.8cm anti-aircraft fire.

British Spitfires in low-level flight harried every German troop movement in the winding roads.

A Ju 88 aircraft has been shot at and set on fire at Marina Dux airfield in Catania. The fire is extinguished with Tutogen foam.

German motor ambulances bring the wounded through war-torn streets to the main field dressing station, always in danger of being strafed by low-flying aircraft.

After its return to the Italian mainland, the Machine Gun Battalion is inspected in Calabria by Field Marshal von Kesselring, commander of German forces in the south, and by the Commander of 1 Parachute Division, Generalmajor von Heidrich. With steel helmet, Battalion Commander Major Werner Schmidt.

Southern Italy 1943

In the Calabretto region as part of 1 Parachute Division.

In the Cosenza area as Battle Group Cosenza under the leadership of Major Schmidt:

Para Machine Gun Battalion
Para Engineer Battalion
1 Para Armoured Battalion
1 Para Medical Company 7
1 Battery 8.8 Flak

Objective: to secure all strategic roads for the withdrawal of units still in the south.

The battle group is placed under the command of the Panzer Corps.

14 August. The Company is assigned its bivouac sites and we pitch camp. Ten minutes away from us in the valley there's a stream with a wonderful little pool, so deep that we can dive into it from two metres above. Our days are spent cleaning our gear and weapons and on recce patrols. In the evening we're spending time with the little group round the Commander, but to be honest I find the excessive drinking that goes on there very hard to accept.

18 August. The Divisional Commander, Generalleutnant Heidrich, greets the Battalion on its return to the mainland. In his address he stresses the fact that, for the first time in the war to date, two opposing parachute units had found themselvs in direct opposition in Sicily. He also congratulates the Battalion on its superb performance during the disengagement. Our Commander, Major Schmidt, is awarded the Knight's Cross in special recognition of the performance of the Battalion. A great honour for us all. And lucky for him that he has such good officers, NCOs and men.

19 August. At 08.30 hours, Company Commanders discussion concerning our imminent transfer to Cosenza (northern Calabria). At 11.00 hours the order comes through for the immediate withdrawal of 1 and 4 Companies and the Staff. Everything is made ready at top speed, packed and loaded. At 14.15 hours the whole

mob, with four Italian lorries, moves out. We travel through Amato to the coast road to Locri, and bivouac about 80 kilometres north.

20 August. At 05.40 hours we move on again, through Squilacce and Stallett to the east coast. The road here winds steeply up to Catanzaro, to the assembly point. The Company reaches it at 16.30 hours and we start preparing for a slightly longer stay. At 17.30 hours Oberleutnant Gehrt – our dentist – arrives with a whole sackful of post. Post from home – that magic word, that dream, made reality again by letters. A quarter of a sack for my mob alone. For me person- ally, 28 letters. Dewes, the eternal civilian, holds the record with 31. Naturally, everyone dives on the post whilst the work – well, that can wait until morning for once. My girl has sent me so many things that I'm speechless and won't be able to answer until morning.

22 August. Planes arrive – and in what numbers! Four waves of twelve twin-engined bombers of American construction roar past, only about 800 metres above, and bomb Cosenza. We can see columns of smoke rising from the town. The anti-aircraft fire is pathetic: there are so few guns that the bombers don't even have to break formation to drop their load. Above them, around 5-8 Spitfires are circling. Our own fighters fail to put in an appearance at all.

23 August. We've become Battle Group Cosenza, which seems to mean that we'll be given another objective in this sector. The assumption proves correct. The task force has the objective of securing the strategic roads against four separate possible enemy attacks, so that the troops in the south can get through to the north without delay. Oberleutnant Dittmar makes a reconnaissance of the area for which the task force is responsible. An advance company consisting of 4 and 1 Companies, a platoon of anti-tank soldiers and a platoon of engineers is placed under Dittmar's command. Leader of the infantry spearhead is Leutnant Quarch. With luck all this will stay in the realms of theory and our thrust to the north will be strong enough.

What are we actually doing here? Whatever we do, Tommy will be successful in the south, where the Italians will put up little resistance. And then he'll probably attack round Naples so as to isolate the 'boot' of Italy. Surely it would be better for us to create a strongly defended line further north, which we'd have prospects of holding successfully?

I'm told to be ready to travel with a convoy of lorries to Calabretto and fetch 2 Company back to us. The order comes in the afternoon and I set off with five lorries.

28 August. Delayed somewhat by the Dittmar Company, we leave at 05.20 hours. Our lorries go like the wind, but little Italian kids manage to hang on to them nonetheless. This time we take the shorter route, along the west coast. It's a beautiful drive, roads taking us through the pass to Soveria-Plagiatra. We can already see the open sea. Nittastro lies deep in the valley at our feet. The people here look very attractive in their national costume, the women in black coats, red shirts and white underskirts. Mostly they are barefoot or – more rarely – wear white stockings and pointed shoes. The offer us local produce which they carry on their heads by means of a ring on their black hair, which enables them to bear surprisingly heavy loads. Their menfolk, in contrast, wander around looking lazy and complacent.

There are scenes like this throughout Calabria, but especially up to Cosenza, Nikarta and Pizzo. Shortly before Enfernia – Lamezia we're forced to make a detour – and then we see a real mess. Hundreds of bomb craters in the river bed, in the road and on the hillsides. The rail bridge has been destroyed, there are railway sleepers hanging in the air. But they haven't managed to cause a landslide which would have made the road impassable, so we travel on via Mileto – Rosano – Gioja – Tauro – Amoto to our camp site at Calabretto. We have our rations, then Leutnant Scherer gets everything loaded up so that we can set off in the morning without delay. Once everything has been taken care of, we hit the bottle. Scherer, Mislowiki, Wasgow and myself, drinking Steinhäger schnapps from water glasses. It's hopeless. Despite the excellent sausage I've eaten, I'm completely knackered by 17.00 hours. My friends carry me to my hammock and I sleep deeply until the early hours, when the racket made by the doctor wakes me up.

We move off punctually, travelling in two separate convoys now with me in the first, quicker one. Back along the same route, without being held up and without coming under attack from the air. Our part of the convoy gets back at 13.00 hours, but the last vehicles from 2 Company don't arrive until 20.00 hours. The equipment and weapons are, once again, in perfect order. Physically, too, we're feeling incredibly refreshed and revitalised by our excellent rations. The day passes quickly.

29 August. The 'paper war' is never-ending. Proposals for promotion, decorations, lists of all kinds are requested without delay. Apparently our little celebrations have been noticed by those

above, so now they're inundating us with so much work that there's hardly any time even for sleep.

More post has arrived, the second lot of the Italian campaign. To great consternation there's none for 1 Company (apart from myself, and I get four letters). But at least our loved ones have had news from Sicily at last. That's some consolation, at least they know roughly where we are.

Oberleutnant Belter has already told me about an imminent transfer to the Tarent sector, and now the Commander has confirmed it. It's proposed that we move on the second or third of September. The American bombers pay us another visit in the afternoon – 48 in number, and escorted by a swarm of fighters. Our flak is completely powerless as they drop their bombs over Cosenza.

The warning order for the transfer of the Battalion to the Altaveruna sector at Tarent has arrived. No further information yet.

3 September. At 09.00 hours, 48 enemy bombers with fighter protection fly overhead again. In the meantime a radio message has been received from 19 Armoured Corps, saying that 2 Battalions of Anglo-American troops landed at Reggio last night. A convoy along the east coast is apparently approaching Locri. Now we're in the firing line again. They'll meet very little resistance in the south, where they face only a few of our units and the Italians are only too keen to surrender, the cowardly pack. 18.15 hours Company discussion, 19.50 hours discussion of the journey to the new sector.

The Battalion is to travel in the following order: 3 Company – 2 Company – Staff – 4 Company – me at the rear.

4 September. As ordered, the first units move off at 06.30 hours. The journey takes us through Cosenza – Tarsia to the east coast. Because we've taken one of 4 Company's lorries in tow, we're soon on our own. But it's a fantastic journey, a real Strength Through Joy outing. Until we reach the coast the road is fairly flat, leading through green-wooded meadows. The coast road itself is nothing special, its main feature being a permanent haze of dust. One valley follows another, with broad riverbeds that are almost dried up, and long bridges. Here and there we come across a 'Zone militare', but these Italian coastal defences are a mixture of joke and bluff. Their trenches and machine-gun nests are nothing short of pathetic when you examine them. The countryside becomes very like the steppes, like the Pussta we remember from our time in Hungary. At 16.00 hours we reach our camp site about 30 kilometres south-west of

Altamura. The Company bivouacs under olive trees on the Casa Iruna estate.

6 September. At 07.00 hours there's a Company Commanders' discussion on the subject of our welcome for Field Marshal Kesselring. At 09.00 hours the Battalion falls in, at 10.30 hours the Field Marshal arrives with General Heidrich. Kesselring congratulates the Battalion on its military successes on Sicily, but his speech is hollow and empty and leaves all of us very disappointed. We expected something better from a Field Marshal. It's simply unbelievable, the rubbish he talks about 'the Italians being good comrades in arms'. I can't stop myself from making a comment and am duly reprimanded, being no more than a callow young Leutnant. At 14.30 hours there's a Company Commanders meeting to discuss the new situation. The Battalion objective is to secure the area round Monte Soaglioso to the south and south-east, and to prevent airborne landing operations by the enemy.

We are all delighted to receive a letter from our Company Commander, Hauptmann Laun, written on 2 September from a military hospital at home. Before that, we hadn't heard from him since he fell ill and was sent to military hospital in Sicily. He writes to the Company.

'To 1 Company – my comrades.

I have followed your struggle on Sicily with pride, but also with great anxiety. Yesterday I received confirmation, at last, that the Battalion and with it yourselves had crossed safely over the Straits of Messina to the mainland. I know that each of you has done his duty to the full and that you are now waiting for the enemy with unbroken spirit in your new positions. Whilst you are doing your duty as soldiers in the south, at home there are heavy burdens to be borne. For the most part these are borne courageously, though there are also many people who are beginning to grow soft. But I have found that the word of a soldier still means something at home. People take heart from our conduct, our words and deeds give them strength to bear the difficult times. That means that all of us must be harder and stronger than other people. We can do this because of our achievements and our responsibility towards our fallen comrades. Our strength, our readiness for sacrifice and action and our unbroken will to victory must be reflected both in our deeds and in our conduct towards home. Remember my words, of which I remind you once again:

> If one of us should doubt
> the other laughs trustingly

and all of you be assured that my most earnest wish is for the day when I can be with you all again.'

Yes, that's typical of our Commander. We all wish him a speedy recovery and a swift return to us.

The people here are reserved and are certainly glad that their war has ended. The Fascists claimed they wanted to fight for the Italian State to the last man, but this looks like hot air. First of all, hardly any efforts are being made to improve the defences. The Italian soldiers have five rounds of ammunition per man, that's all.

We come to a stop some ten kilometres north of Matera. The Battalion does an about-turn and pitches camp five kilometres to the north, in order to wait for further orders from the officer courier. The Tommies have landed at Tarent, so things should be livening up a bit. Rumours and conjectures are multiplying. Then at 14.00 hours the order comes through for us to return to our old sector – this is a crazy war, and our superiors seem to be in a complete flap. We've hardly reached our old camp when, at 16.15 hours, the order comes through for yet another transfer. Then at 16.20 hours an order from the Adjutant, according to which the Company is to remain at Montescaglioso station to guard the road to the south and west. A 5cm anti-tank gun is detailed to us for the purpose. The position is excellent, but unfortunately at 18.00 hours another order comes thorugh: 'Return to Battalion'. Then there's an officers' discussion there. The whole thing is crazy. It's almost beyond believe – we're being sent back to our old sector, and with our old objective!

The Division has the task of securing the left flank of the 76 Armoured Corps, returning from the south. It seems almost funny at first, but the joke wears off slowly.

At 20.30 hours I'm shown round the positions by Oberleutnant Dittmar, to whom I'm again subordinated. The Company takes up position at the Montescaglioso – Potenta – Ginosa road fork and an advanced cyclist guard is posted at 15.00 hours. The night passes quietly and without enemy activity.

11 September. To find out more about the enemy positions I go with my Company messenger Böhnke by solo motorcycle towards Ginosa. Nothing to be seen, though the town is full of angry people as we travel through.

We carry on towards the coast, since Tommy must surely be somewhere around. For a long time we ride down that straight road with nothing to be seen. But there – about 800 metres ahead, and nearly at the coast road, there's a dark spot on the left side of the road. Road block or anti-tank gun? It's unlikely that any of our own troops could be so far forward, so we move cautiously closer. At 500 metres I can clearly make out a gun and about 15 to 20 men standing nearby.

With field glasses I can see a man, naked from the waist up, with his own field glasses trained in our direction. Apart from that we can't make anything out clearly. We move to within 300 metres, when a jeep suddenly roars out of a sidestreet towards us. Shit and damnation – our engine conks out. A quick push, on to the pillion and head back towards our own lines. A wild chase ensues. The Tommies follow us for two or three kilometres, bullets whizzing past. These land to the left, the right and just in front of us – but to our good fortune, their aim is poor and we aren't hit.

Now the engine packs up altogehter. Off and hurl ourselves into the ditch, submachine guns at the ready – but where are they? When the dust settles a bit, we realise that they've turned back. An enormous piece of luck for us, since there's little we could have done against four men armed with a machine-gun. The motorcycle has had it, a ricochet has destroyed the engine. Taking the petrol can with us we set off on foot, completely on our own. Soon a horse and cart appears, so we commandeer it and set off to Ginosa at a lively trot. There, with a little persuasion, we exchange it for two bicycles and return to the Company after our enjoyable little adventure. Message to Oberleutnant Dittmar that the road from Ginosa to the coast is still not occupied by the enemy.

11.15 hours. Order from the Battalion, the lorries have to be cleared out. It's with great distress that I'm parted from my charming and comfortable furniture. At 16.00 hours we're sent mines so we can install some litte traps for the Tommies. Our men lay mines in a kind of chequerboard. Meanwhile, the little bridge is being prepared for demolition, along with the big bridge over the Balka at Casa Irene. I organise a trip to Matera in an effort to find more lorries, but without success.

Eight weeks have passed since the operation in Catania, and Tommy has used it well.

06.00 hours. Idzykowski's scouting party sets out to recce the enemy positions round Ginosa, but turns back at 09.00 hours without sighting the enemy. At 13.30 hours the Italian soldiers and Carabinieri still on Montescaglioso are disarmed. The naval warning station is destroyed. In the meantime, four twin-engined twin-boom aircraft fly over our positions from east to west. The process of disarming the Italians goes without a hitch. There's a whole crowd of people around, of course, but fortunately everything stays quiet.

There's no sound of battle anywhere. From the Battalion we get the order to find our own supplies, since no further rations will be arriving. They don't have to tell us twice: consequently, for breakfast we have half a chicken, a lightly boiled egg, white bread and jam. Needless to say, it goes down very well.

The telephone lines are cut and road signs taken down to make things as difficult as possible for the enemy. We've plenty of time for that.

15 September. At 02.00 hours there's light machine gun fire from the east. Then at 12.00 hours ten twin-engined American bombers roar over our positions, only 2500 metres above us and steering an E-NW course. At 15.30 hours two enemy reconnaissance aircraft pass overhead at a height of 600 metres, turning away to the north west. Enemy bomber and reconnaissance activity has been increasing over the last few days. So has the sun: it's damned hot under the little bridge, like it was on Simeto.

16 September. We're woken at 07.00 hours by nine fighter bombers, but they just fly overhead. Leutnant Wick arrives to pass some time with us. More supplies have arrived at last, enough to last for five days. Obergefreite Martin, who left us in Sicily, arrives back. Naturally enough we're all delighted to see him and there's much laughter as he tells us how he reported back from leave to the Commander, wearing flyers' walking-out uniform, long pants and carrying a case.

17 September. At 08.00 hours, nine fighter bombers overhead again, this time steering a SE-NW course. Before that, Sänger's recce patrol from 2 Company has gone into the hills towards Ginosa to recce the enemy positions. On his return at 10.15 hours he reports that Ginosa and the hills to the south west of the town have been occupied by the enemy. On the road from Ginosa to the coast he saw

big clouds of dust and heard the noise of track-laying vehicles. The recce patrol actually came under fire from a scout car but there were no casualties.

At 07.30 hours, orders from the Battalion arrive. 1 Company is to provide a motorcycle and a soldier with submachine gun, plus a machine gun and crew, for a special mission under Feldwebel Riess. 15.30 hours: five fighter bombers overhead, height approximately 600 metres. 17.00 hours: Idzykowski's recce patrol sets off for the hills in front of Ginosa. He reports back at 21.30 hours with the following observations: enemy not to be seen, but they have observed flash signals from Montescaglioso in the direction of the coast, also from other directions to the coast. It seems fairly certain: the Italians are betraying us. 22.00 hours. Obergefreite Höhnke and Janner report back from the Riess mission. The town of Bernalda has been occupied by the enemy.

18 September. Since the early hours there have been numerous enemy reconnaissance missions using fighter bombers.

11.15 hours. Warning order for withdrawal of the positions to the station, a task completed at 19.00 hours. 13.30 hours – another 12 fighter bombers 500 metres overhead. They're flying wherever they want, without any of our own aircraft putting in an appearance. At 15.30 hours I go with Oberleutnant Dittmar in my little sports car to the Commander. We're told that 1 and 4 Companies are to prepare immediately for transfer to the sector west of Grassano. Objective: to secure the south-west flank of the Battalion.

19.00 hours. The positions are evacuated and, at 19.40 hours, the bridges demolished. The big one needs two charges, twelve metres apart, to bring it down. Our engineers Dietrich and Grimm have done their job well.

22.00 hours. We are moving towards Potenza. Apparently the enemy is already on this road, so things could get quite lively. I ride ahead on the motorcycle, submachine gun on my lap, signal pistol in my hand ready to fire, with 'red' in the barrel. It's a moderately moonlit night, so we make good progress and reach our new positions (the road fork Potenza – Irisina – Matera) at 24.00 hours without coming into contact with the enemy. Messenger Bökhnke turns back immediately to make his report to the Commander.

At 01.30 hours Oberleutnant Dittmar travels through with 4 Company, on their way to secure another strategic road from the south some twenty kilometres westwards. At 04.50 hours we're allocated a 7.5cm antitank gun and move it into position at once.

Feldwebel Jetter takes up position with the strengthened Idzykowsky team. Juba's recce patrol leaves, with the task of blowing up the bridge at Grassano. At 08.00 hours I ride ten kilometres by motorcycle to the demolition area, again without sighting the enemy. The demolition is completed at midday – the bridge has a hole in it some ten metres across.

13.30 hours. Radio message from the Battalion: lorries will be arriving today and continuing on to Rome. They can also take equipment and post. Oberleutnant Dittmar is to be informed.

13.40 hours. Radio message from the Battalion that the position in the town is under attack. 13.45 hours: the Battalion is being attacked from the front, the Staff has dispersed, and we are to report back when Major Schmidt arrives. We ourselves are to march through Matera. Another radio message at 15.15 hours: attack beaten off, another 'walk' is to be prepared, signed Belter. The Commander arrives at 15.30 hours and withdraws to Miglioniki after assessing the latest developments. At 19.00 hours the engineers mine the road from Grassano station to the crossroads. Oberleutnant Dittmar brings important messages from Potenza, which is occupied by Major Böhmler. The night passes quietly.

20 September. Feldwebel Riess, on his way to the Regiment as liaison officer, has breakfast with me and brings the order that 4 Company is to withdraw and take up position here immediately. I also have an interesting conversation with a Canadian prisoner Riess brought with him. A pleasant little chap, twenty-three years old. He claims they are by no means hungry for battle and don't know why they are fighting. At 12.30 hours 4 Company arrives and at 13.10 the covering party from the big bridge at Potenza comes in. The bridge hasn't been blown up, God knows why not. The Battalion is on the move again. 3 and 2 Companies and the Staff are moving straight through to Irisina. Klontz platoon is preparing a covering position north of the riverbed. This night also passes quietly and without enemy activity.

21 September. 05.35 hours. Order from the Battalion: 1 and 4 Companies to move to Irisian immediately – road demolitions – Schmidt.

06.15 hours. 4 Company moves through and we follow five minutes later. All demolitions are completed successfully. We reach Irisian at 07.45 hours. For the moment our Company is to act as Battalion reserve and its only task is to man an observation post. In the course of the day we manage to get hold of an old Ford and a

175cc motorcycle. 18.00 hours. Order from the Battalion: prepare a group with a lorry for use by Hauptmann Frömming.

18.45 hours. Order via Feldwebel Riess: 'Prepare – Good Hunting', then at 22.15 hours a Company Commanders discussion followed by the order to move out immediately – 1 and 2 Companies, Staff, then 3 and 4 Companies. At 24.00 hours I move out at the head as far as the railway bridge. The Battalion assembles at 01.00 hours and I travel on ahead again.

22 September. After a thoroughly exhausting journey over field tracks, the Battalion reaches its new positions at 05.30 hours and bivouacs. On the way, I completely lost my bearings with my luxury car and almost landed up right in the middle of the Tommies. At the last moment I started feeling uncomfortable, so I turned round and eventually found my way back to the Battalion. Though I was able to deliver a valuable situation report after my escapade, I'd like to have killed the guide, the ass. What would have happened to me if the other vehicles had been following hard on my heels? Here at Minervino we have what's more or less a reserve position with the job of guarding the east and north-east flanks of the Regiment. 09.45 hours. Order from the Battalion: 1 and 4 Companies to occupy positions north of Minervino and keep cover to the north and north-west, also to recce in these directions. Unteroffizier Schuhmann is ordered to go on to Canosa by motorcycle to discover enemy movements, preparations for demolition, possibilities for road blocks and mines. Unfortunately the motorcycle breaks down so 4 Company does the job. 18.30 hours. Company Commanders discussion on the new situation. The Battalion objective remains the same: to keep the right flank of the Schulz battle group free and to block the roads from the east. Increased reconnaissance is needed in this direction.

23 September. 02.30 hours – everything's been mucked up yet again – now Oberleutnant Dittmar has to give me new orders. According to his information, the Division has been moving northwards since yesterday. Now the Company's objective is to guard and secure the crossroads three kilometres west of Minerva, as well as the railway crossing. Jetter takes the crossroads, getting an antitank gun for the job, whilst Idzykowski guards the crossing – we have very few men at our disposal now. No enemy activity detectable. We find a good Fiat in a churchyard and manage to get it mobile by evening. At 17.30 hours the order comes to transfer the Company at 19.45 hours and push through to the Minervino –

Canosa – Andria road fork. The Company departs in good time and waits four hundred metres north of the river bridge. Leutnant Scherer has had a long wait for me before blowing up the bridge. Yet again, we're the last ones to arrive. Then off again. We soon reach the Battalion, waiting at the road fork. The first unit moves out at 22.00 hours. Travelling is easy tonight on this wonderful wide asphalt road. Our route leads via Canosa – Carignola to the Ascoli – Satriano sector, which we reach at 05.00 hours.

24 September. It's already light so we can tend to our vehicles properly. 4 Company moves into a huge estate. We're all dog-tired and sleep through till midday. To our great amusement our best organiser and fixer, Unteroffizier Schuhmann, arrives with two carts full of supplies. He's got absolutely everything – flour, noodles, sugar, wine, cigarettes. Everyone starts frying food, roasting chickens etc. At 15.00 hours we're ordered to set up outguards, which we've naturally done long since. At last, after so long, there's time for a game of skat with Leutnants Scherer and Wick. It's a companionable evening.

26 September. At 06.00 hours, as it begins to grow light, I get the guns and the men into position. From 07.45 hours to 08.00 hours, enemy fighter bombers in low-level flight come in to attack the roads north-west of Ascoli with bombs and aircraft armament, managing to set on fire a lorry with its ammunition. At 08.00 hours we can hear the noise of anti-tank or armour-piercing shells in the north-east. At 12.15 hours Oberleutnant Dittmar comes under fire from two English armoured cars in Storranelle, presumably scout cars. At 15.00 hours there's another shooting incident involving local civilians. At first we hadn't a clue what was happening. Then Sergeant Riess advanced with some men from Staff and just shot at anything that moved.

At 17.30 hours Unteroffizier Schuhmann reports three lorries and about 100 Tommies some two kilometres to the north-west. At 18.00 hours four English armoured cars, Supple type, feel their way forward against my left flank, but 800 metres ahead of us they veer away and turn back. Idzykowski's gun crew fires on them with heavy machine-guns, bringing the last vehicle to a halt and making its occupants jump out, cursing and swearing. I quickly put together an assault party, advance rapidly, manage to hold the Tommies at bay and seize the little vehicle. Oberleutnant Dittmar's driver brings it back to our lines. Now we've got ourselves a fast little vehicle, a first-class cross-country car with a twin-barrelled machine-gun at the front and a super-heavy 15mm machine-gun at the rear. We're delighted with our motorised reinforcement. At 18.00 hours, another order for 'good hunting' comes through. The Battalion is to move today to a new line at Deliceto. We move out at 22.00 hours and the Company closes up with the Battalion. 2 Company and the anti-tank artillery come under heavy fire while travelling through the town, and hand grenades are thrown at them. In return, at 01.00 hours 48 shells are fired at Ascoli in a reprisal attack. I remain with the Company and a 5cm anti-tank gun as a combat outpost west of Ascoli. Ascoli.

27 September. In the early morning we occupy our new positions. Vigilance is the order of the day, since Tommy is hard on our heels. From this spot we can control all the approach roads from the east – that's just our little Company and one anti-tank gun! But I have to admit that any attempt to withdraw could get damned tricky. Consequently I've only kept the ambulance, a motor cycle and my little car here. At 18.00 hours I travel to Delicedo to recce the route. The path is so bad that whenever possible I travel right on the road although it means that I have to move right along the front line for 15 kilometres.

At 10.45 hours, up in the town, a crowd of people start milling around – then who should come down? It's the Bishop of Ascoli, to make excuses for the goings on of the previous night. After much haggling I impose a fine of 1000 cigarettes and 50 kilograms of bread on the town, to be delivered by 15.00 hours.

At 11.30 hours two German lorries and their crew set off in the direction of Canacia. Slowly but surely the weather is changing. We're at the beginning of the rainy season and the sky is full of dark clouds, although it isn't raining just yet. At least these conditions are more tolerable than the baking heat of the last few weeks.

At 12.15 hours we can make out great movements of people at the edge of the town. Aha – our cigarettes and food are on their way. Just think, in the meantime the Tommies had arrived in the town, travelling in two little armoured personnel carriers as far down as the station. We didn't stir and after half an hour they turned back again. At 13.10 hours another armoured scout car appeared. It got closer and closer to us. Now there was no prospect of us hiding any longer, so out with the antitank gun. The second shot was a direct hit, setting the vehicle on fire. For the time being, things are quiet again.

At 17.00 hours I meet Leutnant Stahl of the Army Engineers on the road. They have been given the job of laying stray mines during the night. Much pleasure in seeing him. We finally leave at 18.50 hours and at 20.00 hours we make contact with 4 Company on the road. I make my report to the Battalion over the radio and am ordered to push on to the Battalion, without the anti-tank gun. The Battalion is supposed to be moving again tonight but – though it's almost midnight already – they haven't received their orders yet. Now it's getting more spooky, since we're totally alone in the open countryside. The roads on which we're due to be withdrawing may have been occupied by the enemy since yesterday, the Commander reckons. At last the order to withdraw comes through, so at 04.45 hours we're huddled over the maps with the Commander. We're to travel through Bovino-Orsara in the following order: 3 Company – Staff – 1 Company – 2 and 4 Companies. At 07.30 hours we arrive, without making into contact with the enemy.

28 September. Our new positions, though relatively favourable in some circumstances, simply cannot be held in the face of major enemy attack. In the afternoon, some Tommies and an armoured scout car are observed at Castell Lucia. A motorcycle messenger from the Staff comes under fire in the town. Our hunch that we won't be staying here for long either is confirmed at 18.15 hours, when the order comes through to withdraw at 18.50 hours. Get a move on! The positions are quickly evacuated, with only Schröder staying behind to provide cover. An assault party from 4 Company comes back without success. At 21.00 hours the Battalion moves out. Yet again I have the pleasure of bringing up the rear and reporting to the engineers as soon as the Battalion is through. In the south-west there is so much thunder and lightning that it looks as if there were a battle going on. The sky is dreadfully dark, the road extremely twisting and narrow. Added to that, the lightning is so dazzling that I remark to my assistant driver that we'll be very lucky to escape an accident. Almost immediately a heavy lorry carrying a 7.5cm anti-tank gun overturns. Wounded men are crying out and groaning, but at least it wasn't the last vehicle in the convoy. I race past the other vehicles to the front to fetch the ambulance and report to the Adjutant, then turn back again. We get the wounded out and I know I'll have to borrow a lorry from the engineers so we can get the crashed vehicle upright and operating again. Now it's raining here as well. An inadequate description – it's coming down in buckets. Everything is soaked within seconds, down to the last rag, and with water running down our goggles it's well-nigh impossible to see anything. We struggle on and finally reach the large, wide main road. There we're

dogged by more bad luck when our vehicle breaks down – water must have got into the engines. Fortunately there's a farmstead nearby where we can stop and put it right. The excellent Kehls takes only a quarter of an hour to get the car going again. He's a real expert, that fellow. In the meantime a bottle of herbal liquor does sterling service, as we're all shivering from the cold and wet. Instead of the engineers, we come across 10 Company from 3 Regiment who have taken up position here. I borrow an Opel Blitz and we soon get the big lorry clear. Slowly, we make our way down the twisting road, with the rain still pouring down. At 02.00 hours we reach the Battalion near Roseto.

29 September. Our clothes are still soaked and clinging to our bodies, so I take my chance to get into the ambulance and cover myself with warm blankets. Ahead of us we can see vehicles still stuck in the mud, preventing us from driving on. At last they're all cleared out of the way and we're on our way again. Meanwhile Jetter has been receiving our orders and has been shown the boundaries of our new positions. By 14.00 hours we have moved into them and set up the Company command post in the town hall. After a long day, at least we've found decent quarters.

At 18.00 hours Leutnant Scherer brings the order: 1 Company to send a stationary patrol to the village of Stella, about five kilometres from here. In the event of contact with the enemy, patrol to feign strength by means of a short concentration of fire, then to withdraw. Obergefreite Kretschmar goes with them. For the time being we're very comfortable in our club room with its leather furniture. Weber heats up the room a bit, whilst Franz disappears into the kitchen to conjure up a decent pancake. Like a first class restaurant, really. The people here are thoroughly peacable so we get on well. Understandably enough, they've hidden everything away, but I'm afraid we can't have any regard for that. We take what we need, though no more than that.

30 September. That was a fantastic night, quiet and peaceful. Then a shining blue morning, with the sun seeming to bless us. One of those mornings that are never bettered, that make you want to celebrate and forget this whole murderous business that's swamping the world. But then the recce patrol leader arrives back, reminding me of grim reality – we're all ordinary soldiers and are likely to remain so for some time. The village of Stella is still free of the enemy, a fact I report to the Commander. But what's this? I can hardly believe my eyes, because here comes Hauptmann Hirsch with our

lively little Inspektor Jost. I'm absolutely delighted to see the little fellow again. To our even greater joy they have post with them, the fourth of this campaign. At 16.45 hours another warning order for 'good hunting' comes through. It's enough to make you puke – the minute things get a bit better they send us off on our travels again. How far will it be this time? As far as the Brenner Pass, or all the way to Munich? We're to move out at 19.00 hours, but one of our recce patrols hasn't got back yet. It eventually arrives at 19.45 hours and we move out. We reach Bartholomeo at 01.30 hours and stop there, sleeping beside our vehicles.

1 October. Oberleutnant Dittmar and I tour the new sector. After much discussion we agree to move into positions close by the road, hoping that the Commander will allow himself to be convinced it's the right decision. It's our Commander's birthday today, so my last sausage and the last bottle of Vermouth are sacrificed for a present. However, we're all happy that we can give the 'Old Man' something, at least.

Increased alert at 16.00 hours, since fifteen tanks have been seen in Voturino. I send Idzykowski with a scouting party to find out the exact location of the tanks. At 18.30 hours we get the order for the next 'good hunting'. The lorries are moved up. Leutnant Wick takes charge of the anti-tank artillery and covers the road fork at Coltuara.

18.45 hours. Recce patrol reports tank advance from the direction of Motta towards the hills north-east of Voltuara. Our own infantry is engaged in combat against enemy infantry and armoured units, with artillery fire from both sides. 19.30 hours – Battalion withdraws in teeming rain and fog in the direction of Voltuara – Cambaltesa. About three kilometres west of Voltuara, we stay in reserve. My Company is placed under the command of the Grassmehl Battalion. Under artillery fire, I arrive at the crossroads north-west of Motta at 11.30 hours and report to Major Grassmehl. The entire sector and the roads have been subjected to artillery bombardment throughout that morning. At midday eleven enemy Mark IIIs and other tanks move out of Motta and come to a halt some 2500 metres from us. Then six tanks and accompanying infantry begin their attack. We open fire at 800 metres, hitting five tanks and setting them ablaze. The other manages to get away. Three cheers for our anti-tank gunners!

It's a pity that I don't have my heavy machine-guns here (the Company is still on the way here using mule transport). For the moment, we devote all our efforts to providing some kind of cover in the hard stone, at least some shallow hollows. The artillery activity increases slowly. At 16.00 hours some British infantry manage to work their way slowly towards us. But our heavy machine guns have arrived by now, and we use these and our 2cm flak to such effect that they're forced to withdraw with their wounded. At 17.00 hours things really start to hot up. There's a magnificent artillery show put on, but unfortunately not for our benefit. Our right sector comes under increasing fire. It's possible to make out the muzzle flashes of at least 28 guns of up to 15cm calibre. In the right sector, the bombardment increases until it becomes a murderous barrage, just like on Simeto in Sicily. The batteries are lined up in four rows, spitting lead and death at our hills. Our poor comrades over there have all our sympathy.

At 20.00 hours Tommy breaks through on the right flank, capturing a 7.5cm anti-tank gun and other equipment. Fortunately the men manage to seal off the penetration quickly. Two of our men are still missing: Dewes and Grimm. Surely they haven't wandered unsuspectingly into the hands of the Tommies?

At 23.00 hours Obergefreite Böhnke brings the order to withdraw alongside Meier's Company at 00.15 hours. Quickly and silently we move to the lorry assembly point about three kilometres from here and then drive away without mishap, although it's already begun to bucket down again, damn it! It's not far this time though, and as I'm posted back to Battalion I get there in the early morning. For now, we're to remain in reserve.

3 October. At first we all huddle round a crackling fire in a big barn. The warmth is wonderful, spreading through bones and sinews. Lots of men are playing skat, but soon, one after another, they crawl into the straw to sleep. Schuhmann's gun crew takes up position on the hill some 500 metres north-east of Casa Cantoniera to provide close-range protection. Our artillery, which has been equipped with Italian 7.5mm infantry howitzers for a number of days now, is firing repeatedly short bursts towards the enemy positions, whilst the enemy artillery is currently restricted to a few sudden concentrations of fire. The day passes relatively quietly. I sleep like a baby in an American sleeping bag that was in the car we captured.

4 October. Nothing is moving and we're glad to get a decent sleep for once. At 06.00 hours our own artillery wakes us with heavy fire on Voltuara. They're at it early, our boys, as though they know that the Tommies like a good long sleep. Blankets over my head, and back to

sleep again. At 08.00 hours I set off to the Commander since it's urgent that I organise supplies for my men behind the lines. The road leads right past Gambaltera, curving steeply down. It's then that I have the most appalling piece of bad luck. In one of the narrow hairpin bends my right wheel hits a milestone and I overturn down an embankment, about 3 metres deep. I'm flung out and struck by the machine as it topples over. It hits me in the pelvis, so that I see a whole skyful of stars. A grab down there reassures me that everything is still there, but the left testicle has been forced out of the sac and is starting to swell and looks a disgusting blue. It's such a damn stupid way for me to be put out of action, especially when the men are having such a hard time. The Commander will surely have something to say about it!

It takes and age until the ambulance gets there. I'm soon loaded in and lying in this hearse, where every jolt sets off new agonies. At Jelci, in the clearing station, I'm stitched up there and then. That same evening, I'm taken by ambulance to the medical collecting station in Rome. Apparently because they're so short of beds, I find myself lying with a whole crowd of others in a Church, near to the High Altar. Next day the orderlies bring in a man on a stretcher, groaning and shivering. To my astonishment it's none other than my old friend and comrade-in-arms from Crete, Leutnant Scherer, who's got a bad dose of malaria. So, not for the first time, we renew our friendship in a clearing station.

We stay in Rome for two days, getting excellent care and food. then we're loaded into an Italian ambulance train and travel via Riccione – Padua – Bad Gastein – Salzburg towards Munich. Scherer has another bad attack on the way, has to be strapped to his bed and, to my great regret, is taken off the train in Rosenheim. Personally I can hardly take it in – the train is going past my home city of Munich – they must be crazy – and travelling on to Lörrach on the Swiss border.

In this way, my own personal Italian campaign came to an end.

On 1 October 1943 I became an Oberleutnant and Company Commander, shortly before my 23rd birthday. That's such an easy thing to write and to read, but what a responsibility for such a young man. Responsibility for 180 men whose parents, wives, fiancées, brothers and sisters and friends are waiting for them, hoping that they will come back at least half-fit and well. In those days I hardly gave it a thought, but now I'm appalled at the deadly 'cops and robbers' game we were ordered to play. Certainly, a man of 30 or 35 has achieved a certain maturity – but a man of 23?

Our Machine Gun Battalion continued to beat a fighting retreat through Italy. The mountainous countryside was favourable to them, making it hard for the Allies to press home the attack. In the region of Monte Cassino the front came to a halt and, after Crete, another heroic chapter in the history of 1 Parachute Division began, in what became the Verdun of the Second World War. Despite the onslaught of many enemy Divisions, of shell fire which frequently lasted all day, despite carpets of bombs, the men held firm, crawled out of their holes and returned the fire. Singly, in pairs, sometimes a few more. Like Crete, this month-long battle took a high toll in the blood of our men. And when the Benedictine monastery of Monte Cassino was finally destroyed by Allied bomber formations, it was the men of the Machine Gun Battalion who were the first to take up a position of all-round defence up there.

What a Parachute Machine-Gun Battalion, and what men.

Normandy 1944 –
The Allied Invasion

I stayed for some weeks in beautiful Lörrach, in its peace and seclusion. Tensely, over the radio and on my map, I follow the battles of 1 Division, which included my Battalion and my Company. The first Battle of Monte Cassino – how have things gone for my comrades, who's been wounded, who else has sacrificed his young life? A desperately hard time for the blokes whilst I'm recovering here. A couple of days of home leave, then at last I leave for the replacement training battalion – I think it was in Oschersleben – and report for duty again. To my delight my old friend and comrade in arms, Leutnant Scherer, is here as well. Both of us are overjoyed at the idea of returning to the unit together – but it wasn't to be.

One of the 'Old Men' is looking for battle-tested and experienced men from among the convalescents for the new 6 Regiment. We do our best to decline, but when he discovers that we're both 'Heavies', from heavy weapons companies, that's it. On the 'highest' orders, we have to join the new 6 Regiment, a rude awakening from our dream of Monte Cassino, from the dream of fighting alongside our friends. Whether we want to or not, we're told to depart for Cologne-Wahn.

In the period between 15 January and 1 May 1944, 6 Parachute Regiment was raised from scratch. Commanding officers and prospective officers were drawn largely from paratroopers of the Parachute Training Battalion. Old names appeared, such as Hauptmann Trebes, Hauptmann Bartelmes and that old campaigner Oberleutnant Wagner, holder of the Wound Badge in gold. All three of these men were holders of the Knight's Cross.

The squad is composed of young volunteers from the Luftwaffe and Anti-Aircraft Artillery, who are incredibly committed to our branch of the service. At the beginning the Regiment is very lively with everyone, especially the young soldiers, still having a mind and opinions of his own. However, this assorted bunch is gradually being turned into a Regiment which will be a match for whatever demands are made of it. At the end of April 1944 the Regiment leaves for France to take up position ready for an enemy invasion in the West.

6 Regiment and its Task

(6 Parachute Regiment under the command of Major Freiherr von der Heydte, holder of the Knight's Cross, was deployed in the Carentan-Le Plessie region at the start of the Anglo-American invasion, and for tactical purposes was assigned to 91 Airborne Division.)

Objective: to secure the combat sector against enemy airborne operations.

Command of the Regiment:	Major Freiherr von der Heydte
Adjutant:	Hauptmann Peisser
I Battalion:	Hauptmann Preikschat
II Battalion:	Hauptmann Mager
III Battalion:	Hauptmann Trebes
Command of III Battalion:	Hauptmann Trebes
Adjutant:	Leutnant Treuherz
ADC:	Oberleutnant Ulmer
Signals Officer:	Oberleutnant Seibert
9 Company:	Oberleutnant Wagner
10 Company:	Oberleutnant Prive
11 Company:	Oberleutnant Märk
12 Company:	Oberleutnant Pöppel
Command of 12 Company:	Oberleutnant Pöppel
Company Sergeant Major:	Oberfeldwebel Helbig
I Platoon:	Oberfeldwebel Peters
II Platoon:	Oberfeldwebel Rentsch
III Platoon:	Feldwebel Honig
IV Platoon:	Leutnant Schröder
V Platoon:	Oberfähnrich Doppelstein

The Regiment takes up position in the Carentan-Le Plessie region. Each battalion forms a subsector, taking responsibility for observation and defence in its own area. Special care has to be taken to secure the regions which seem particularly favourable for an airborne landing operation by the enemy. In our sector, there are two such areas. Firstly, the region to the south of Carentan, a piece of countryside about two kilometres long and one kilometre wide, completely flat and without vegetation. Around this landscape there are flat elevations from which the whole sector can be controlled.

The second such area lies between Carentan and Periers, a long, thin strip of land which is particularly suitable for troop-carrying gliders.

The Regiment with all its units, is established in its field positions, which we have worked tirelessly to complete. Alarm exercises by day and by night increases our combat readiness. The whole terrain has been surveyed for the heavy weapons, almost every eventuality has been considered. On 3 June there is further regrouping as a result of the flooding of some parts of the countryside. The command post of the heavy weapons is transferred to St Georges de Bohon, observation posts being established in the Church tower. More arduous labour to extend the positions, put up camouflage nets and set up sniper's posts. Then the Regiment can wait calmly for the expected attack from the enemy. On 5 June a map exercise is carried out involving all the Battalion's officers and platoon leaders, in which the possibilities of an airborne landing by the enemy are played through. We disperse amid laughter and no one has any idea how near we are to the real situation. Only a few hours later all our preparations are to be put to the test.

5 June. I've set up my Company HQ in a Normandy farmhouse, and it's really homely and snug with the warmth of the open fire lit by my batman Söser. It's nearly midnight and I'm about to take off some clothes and get some sleep when the leader of my company headquarters personnel, flat-headed Feldwebel Behne, rouses me with the words 'Herr Oberleutnant, shall I open another bottle of fizz?' I laugh at this crazy idea but am happy to give him permission because he is definitely on edge, feeling that something is going to happen today.

Outside the bombing is still going on. There has recently been an endless wave of attacks by bomber formations on the entire traffic system in France. They drone over our heads in large numbers.

My observation post reports that loud explosions can be heard about 8 kilometres away. We look out but can't see any more than that. Then the Commander calls me as well, wanting to know whether I can make any more precise report. Now more aircraft, damned near this time. The loud explosions must be coming from Carentan itself. It's a restless night. Perhaps old Behne is right, and something is going to happen. As there seems to be no end to the formation of enemy aircraft, I order the company to be ready for action. Once more can't do any harm.

6 June. The bombardment continues. Bombing is reported throughout the area. II Battalion, which is guarding an airfield,

reports bombing by massive enemy formations. We have dressed and are talking uneasily about these developments. Then more aircraft fly over, this time very near and flying low.

02.00 hours. Alarm! The sentries roar the alarm signals through the night. All my observation posts are reporting enemy parachute landings. In an instant we're wide-awake and quickly ready. First orders to the train and telephone central for all-round defence, the first reports to the Commander. Damn, our map exercise has suddenly turned into the real thing.

I hurry to my main observation post with my company HQ personnel. We release the safety-catches on our weapons, but nobody knows exactly where the enemy is yet. According to the reports, there have been parachute drops in the whole area. At the Church tower the first two positive reports reach me. The enemy, with an estimated strength of 2-3 companies, has made a parachute drop over our sector between St Georges de Bohon and Rougeville. As yet, no stronger forces have appeared.

The first wounded prisoners, three Americans, are brought in by 13 Company heavy mortar platoon. The first short interrogation doesn't produce any results, though. The fellows have been well trained and just answer every question by saying: 'I don't know'.

There are single cracks of rifle fire, but so far we have only detected the position of individual enemy soldiers and can't use our heavy guns yet. The night is stormy and wild. From time to time the moon lights up the darkness. No enemy movements can be detected from the Church tower.

04.00. Bombers drone overhead again from the south. When they are directly above, more parachutes come floating down. It all happens so quickly that we scarcely have time to shoot. The chutes disappear rapidly in the thick underbrush of the Normany hedgerows. We respond with machine gun fire, then sub-machine gun and carbine fire towards the enemy, although we aren't sure of his position. More prisoners are brought in, great hulking figures. Is this the American elite? They look as though they could be from Sing-Sing.

Slowly the day breaks, enabling us to survey the terrain through our field glasses. Here and there we can see the parachutes, camouflage colour for the paratroopers, pink for the ammunition and yellow for the weapons. Some soldiers arrive with booty and we all take the opportunity to smoke some American cigarettes. Yet more prisoners come in and we put them in the church for the time being. They are exhausted and completely done in. The altar is transformed into a first-aid station. So far, we have only suffered a few casualties ourselves.

To crown it all, our connections with the Battalion have been broken – probably cut through. But the Commander will already have made his decisiions based on the overall situation, and will be sending reinforcements to comb the countryside.

With the dawn, the enemy begins light mortar fire. Without doubt it's aimed at our Church tower, the only good observation point in the entire area. The gunner shoots slowly. Lucky for us that he is short of ammunition, or we would soon have had to get out.

06.30 hours. From Rougeville Oberleutnant Prive makes an attack through the open countryside, pushing towards us. We use light signals to show the direction of the enemy. He pushes closer and closer. In copybook fashion – again showing the value of our tough training – his groups advance, one covering and shooting whilst the other moves forwards firing with sub-machine guns from the hip. Then they attack with hand grenades and sub-machine gunfire ripping into the hedgerows. Arms are raised aloft in the thick bushes as the enemy surrenders. A real triumph for Prive, who takes more than sixty American prisoners with a single platoon.

Soon they are standing in front of us, these big fellows from the United States, giants of men with beefy faces. The prisoners include a Captain and several other officers. Their equipment is only of moderate quality in general, but the medical equipment is impressive. Each soldier is carrying morphine and tetanus injections. Of course, their rations also include cigarettes, chocolate, biscuits, coffee and gum. The most comical are the long daggers which each of them carries strapped to his foot or at his belt, just like we have our flick blade knives in the right-hand pocket above the knee.

They walk in long rows into the church since we can't transport them away at the moment. Among them is a pleasant young doctor, a Captain called Thomas Urban Johnson, with whom I find time to talk. (Long after the war his wife told me he had died.) A considerate doctor and a good bloke, as I find out during the short time in the church.

Outside, the battle group of about 100 men is much calmer now that we have taken prisoners. Here and there, more American prisoners come and give themselves up. Our special troops are on their way to mend the broken lines. We can see parachutes hanging and lying all over the area, so we fetch them in and look them over – torn ones are turned into scarves. Of course, we now have vast quantities of cigarettes and chocolate, at least for the time being. At 09.50 hours a messenger from the Battalion Commander arrives ordering us to headquarters to discuss the new situation.

It turns out that this really is the Allies' big day – which unfortunately means that it's ours too. In the Regiment's sector the only airborne landings have been in our sub-sector, so the two other Battalions have been thrown straight in to the coast to join the battle against the Allies there. So far as we can tell, many more enemy airborne troops and landing parties have landed in the Vire-Mündung region. Even bigger units are said to have dropped and landed at St Marie du Mont and I Battalion has gone into action against them. According to various recce reports, the remants of the companies that dropped in our area have withdrawn to the villages at Graignes and Tribehou. To prevent these from attacking us from the rear, our entire Battalion will move against them. The withdrawal of the necessary troops for this purpose, and the continued occupation of the region against further airborne forces, are to be ensured by the following measures:

1. 9 Company – apart from Schenkendorfer platoon, which is to guard the old sub-sector – to advance immediately on a wide front through Sainteny on the main road to St André de Bohon, to comb the countryside and then to return to the rest of the Battalion.

2. 10 Company: Hoppe's platoon to stay by the church, along with Binder's heavy machine-gun group. The rest of the Company to advance to the main road and to stay on guard until all sections of the Battalion have gathered.

3. 11 Company to leave one platoon in its former position, the remainder also to advance to the main road.

4. Each Company to receive one LKW, 12 Company to get two and a motorcycle.

5. Movements to begin immediately, maximum speed.

These movements start immediately after the return of the commanders, but take longer than envisaged because of the difficulties encountered by 9 Company. It advances to Tribehou, keeping guard on all sides, and holds the location against attack. I've put my heavy gun platoon leaders in the picture and the positions have been surveyed. Finally, at 16.00 hours, 9 Company reports in.

16.15 hours. Final discussion of the attack with the Battalion Commander. If the battle for Tribehou-Graignes goes favourably, the Battalion will then advance to the outskirts of Carentan. Once our men are in Tribehou, we are to follow with the heavy weapons.

16.30 hours. Messenger from the Regimental radio section: the Battalion is not attacking after all. Instead, all units are to follow 9 Company to Carentan, where American reconnaissance patrols have been sighted. Further orders to locations from Regimental Commander. So, off we go back again. If it carries on like this, the situation might get difficult. The men are already under considerable strain with the burden of ammunitions and weapons.

9 Company is transferred to Carentan in all available lorries, whilst the Battalion marches there on foot. Finally more vehicles arrive to take my Company back to their old positions. The main effort will again be shifted to the old positions on Hill 30, where I establish my command post.

21.00 hours. Contact is established with 9 Company and we hear that the enemy has still not entered Carentan. The enemy patrols, recognising our temporary superiority, have withdrawn. 9 Company concentrates on all round defence.

22.30 hours. Situation discussion with the Commander.

According to the latest reports from the Regiment, the enemy landing forces are already advancing on St Come-du-Mont. I Battalion has been assigned to engage them, but no reports have been received on its progress so far. We discuss the possibilities of ordering II Battalion to advance in that direction, followed by further reinforcement by III Battalion during the course of the battle.

During the night, aircraft observation posts report continuing overflights by aircraft. I have pitched camp in the open air so that I'll be ready for action at any time. The Company is encamped in the potholes, and is fully prepared for action. These brave lads deserve their sleep – and who knows what the next day will bring? But it's a long time before I manage to grab a little sleep myself. Large fires are visible on the horizon, which must have been caused by bombing by our own aircraft. Whatever success they have comes none too soon, since not a single German aircraft had been spotted that day. Where the hell are they? Every day is absolutely critical. Every day and every night – in fact every hour – the enemy is bringing his reinforcements ashore. Only by destroying the landing craft, the enemy fleet involved in the whole operation, can we destroy the enemy's supplies and give ourselves a chance to drive him back into the sea. Even at this stage, many reinforcements have already got ashore without harassment.

Despite my exhaustion, I find it very difficult to sleep. Everything is still too new, the impressions are still too fresh in my mind to let me drop off. But after a few days of battle we'll all have regained the ability to snatch a little sleep whenever and wherever we can.

When I do finally doze, we're all woken up by a false alarm. Thank heavens, it's not the real thing. That first momentous night passes, and a bright morning dawns. Our tired eyes blink at that bright sky, and at first we can hardly believe that today we'll be at war again. Quickly, all traces of our night's rest disappear so that enemy pilots don't get any check points.

7 June. At first light vast numbers of enemy bombers reappear, bringing death and fire into the French hinterland. Naturally, their targets are the railway junctions, strategic concentration points and channels of communication, as well as our advancing armoured units. They know well enough that if they can eliminate our reinforcements they should be able to achieve their objectives without massive casualties. As for our own pilots – they are nowhere to be seen.

We all reckon that I Battalion has been thrown into battle alone and with no prospects of success. It must already have suffered considerable casualties if it hasn't been wiped out completely – and my friend and comrade Eugen Scherer is with them. During the night, the Regimental Commander has ordered II Battalion to relieve I Battalion. The north-east position of the hills of St Come-du-Mont must be held at all costs, to provide a favourable basis for further counterattacks.

Enormous explosions can be heard in the north and north-east, which must be coming from the enemy's naval heavy artillery. We can also hear the noise of battle from that direction.

13.00 hours. 9 Company has now been moved to St Come-du-Mont to consolidate our positions there.

We have learned that I Battalion has suffered very high casualties after the Americans made further airborne landings by glider to the rear of them in the early hours of the morning. With enemy units ahead of them, with a whole Regiment of elite enemy troops behind them, and with marshland to the south, all that the Battalion could do was to take up a positon of all-round defence and defend themselves to the last man. Meanwhile, II Battalion has gone on the attack in the north, but made only sporadic contact with enemy units and has been forced to withdraw to the hills. There it has been reinforced by a fortress construction battalion composed partly of young and old infantrymen but partly of Russians who can't really be relied on.

During the morning, 9 Company advances as far as the foothills of the mountains but is then forced to yield to the enemy's superior force. The Company is now sealing off the hills alongside units of II Battalion and the infantry.

17.00 hours. On the order of the Battalion, second mortar group under Leutnant Schröder is despatched to reinforce 9 Company. I go with my captured French car and the lorry over the 2 kilometres of marshland to St Come-du-Mond so that I can supply the group myself and can discuss tomorrow's plan of attack with Oberleutnant Wagner.

At Regimental headquarters the order reaches me to prepare tomorrow's attack with Oberleutnant Wagner. The plan is to drive the enemy back to St Marie-du-Mont. In the opinion of the men involved, this task can't be achieved with the forces we have available. The Americans, supported by their naval artillery, are already advancing inexorably and our advanced units are already engaged in bitter fighting. Although night is slowly closing in, there has been no let-up in the noise of battle. With Unteroffizier Hiester and my loyal paladin Söser I go to the front to see Oberleutnant Wagner and discuss the situation with him on the spot.

Despite everything we learned in our peacetime exercises, the men are lying in large groups right next to each other. They can only be dispersed with great difficulty and much profanity. A few hundred metres further on, and the shells are landing close by. At once I'm transported back into the old-style warfare. I come across Wagner behind a hedge, in discussion with the infantrymen. Today he doesn't seem as calm and level-headed as he usually is. Messages continue to come in, bringing important information from the command posts.

After a short time the main points of the attack have been discussed over the map, the ground signals and signals agreed. The leader of his company HQ personnel takes rapid notes and asks some final questions. Then a cry from ahead: enemy attacking with tanks!

The men, particularly the infantrymen, are damned jittery. But even Wagner can't seem to make up his mind what to do. Since I can't help here but can only make things worse, I start to make the journey back with my lads. At the junction I meet my mortar group, which has just got here by truck. Quickly, we organise the unloading of the shells. I give my instructions to Schröder and then travel back in the lorry. The driver races along the narrow dirt road with its high hedgerows like the devil incarnate, and brings us back to Regimental HQ.

A massive operation is under way there. ADCs come and go, messengers hurry past and are quickly dispatched on their way. The lamp is burning in the underground bunker – the Commander and the Battalion Commander are at work. Outside, the soldiers' cigarettes are glowing in the darkness. The Old Man gives Oberleutnant Prive the information about tomorrow's attack, so he discusses the last details with us. He too is less than delighted with the strength of the forces available to him. In particular, he's angry that he has to attack with just two platoons. We can all sympathise with his predicament.

What has persuaded the Commander to depart from the basic principles of his map exercise? Before this he always preached to us to 'Think big!' – but now he's simply tearing this fighting Regiment apart. It's incomprehensible. But perhaps – and more likely – the whole tragedy lay in the fact that the whole Regiment had only about 70 trucks at its disposal, and these were often so old and useless that we couldn't repair them when they broke down. Replacement parts simply weren't available any more. Consequently, most of our elite Regiments had to go everywhere on foot, like in the Middle Ages, carrying all the heavy guns, anti-tank guns and mortars. The General Staff seems to have thought that we paratroopers could manage with nothing more than our knives. This attitude even seems to have affected Field Marshal Rommel, who was otherwise so prudent: he had created defences against airborne landings, had ingeniously strengthened to the coastline – but little or nothing was available for the rapid transportation of the reserve divisions to the coast. On the highest orders, the Waffen SS divisions far behind the coast were actually the best equipped. Consequently, on that first day the writing was already on the wall for our proud 6 Regiment. At the end of these battles – when I was already wounded – it had lost more than three thousand men dead, wounded, missing. A few hundred, I discovered later, managed to get away at the Falaise Gap.

But back to this night: suddenly we recognise the sound of armour-piercing shells nearby. An enemy armoured scout car has broken through to headquarters in a daredevil drive and is now firing across the street, although he can't see a great deal. Tremendous excitement here, much shouting for anti-tank grenade launchers. At last the vehicle is hit by heavy fire. But nobody dares to attack the accompanying infantry, so I get together a couple of soldiers who are standing around and move forward. Everybody is frankly shit-scared in this eerie night, and I have to curse and swear at them to get them to move. When we reach the burning car, from which the ammunition is rattling and exploding heavenwards, we come across a single Yankee, completely shattered by the effect of our fire. He's creeping around in his stockinged feet, in a terrible state. After we've advanced another hundred metres, I realise that this single Ami was responsible for all the panic, and we turn back.

I send out the following orders through the messenger:

1. Company command post to be moved immediately to Carentan church, the main observation post to be established in the tower.
2. Machine-gun platoon Rentsch to move north of Pommenauque, holding position so that it can provide flanking support for Wagner's company when it makes its attack in the early hours.
3. Heavy mortar platoon 13/6 also to move to this area and fulfil the same task.
4. Howitzer platoon to take up position west of Carentan and work out the basic firing distances.

After further discussions with the Regimental Commander I return at 23.00 hours. My orders have by now been carried out, or are still being implemented. Lines to the platoons are being laid by my tireless signals communication men, the observation tower is being prepared and everything is discussed with the platoon leaders for tomorrow's attack. We work on the high tower so that it doesn't look suspicious to the fighter-bombers which will surely reappear tomorrow. Then we try to get a few hours sleep so that we'll be refreshed for the next day.

The night passes quietly and without incident.

8 June. Things get under way before dawn. Only one thing is wrong: it's not our attack, but the enemy's, hitting deep into our assembled troops. The attack begins with sustained bombardment from the enemy naval artillery, explosion after explosion landing on our comrades over there. Using our field glasses and the battery commander's telescope, we try to penetrate the thick mist, but

without success. We can locate the line only roughly by listening for the exceptionally rapid fire of our MG 42s. Our six-barrelled mortars have begun to fire as well, but there's just no comparison with the enemy's armoury of heavy guns.

As the day grows brighter, we can see our targets. At one point there's a large number of Yankees running about, apparently a supply depot or even a command post. Doppelstein soon works out the firing distances, then we send the first shells over. After a few shots, we start to make direct hits. Brick dust whirls upwards from the farmhouse, people come running out in an attempt to get away from concentrated mortar fire. Even the cows are jumping around in comical fashion. Don't forget – we can shoot too.

On the mountains, the sound of battle is moving to the west – which means that we are retreating slowly. If we could only get a signal from the infantry, but there's nothing, absolutely nothing. It makes me want to throw up. We're desperate to help those poor fellows, but when we've no idea where the front line is we can't do a thing. Surely it would be so easy for the infantry to show the position of the front line by sending up a light signal?

It's full daylight now. The enemy's artillery strikes are landing further forward, making thick clouds of smoke drift eastwards over the hedges. More gliders are landing by the church of St Mere-Eglise. We see a lot of them being smashed to pieces on the trees. Then the bomber formations pass overhead again on their way into the hinterland.

09.00 hours. A powerful formation of American fighter-bombers is approaching our town very rapidly. Dammit, if they drop their bombs here, things could get very unpleasant for us as well. But they turn away to the north-east, and then make a dive over the bridges over the Vire canal which is some 1.5 kilometres away from us. Great fountains of water are tossed up by the force of the bombs. Many bombs land directly in the water, creating even more spouts of water. After the spell is broken and the dust has settled, we see that the bridges are bridges no longer. Those boys have done a precision job. But what's that? Along the roadside by the bridge yellow and red cloths have been laid out! Then we recognise the round helmets of the Yankees. Well, they'll have been less than delighted with their comrades in the Air Force, since most of the bombs will have landed right in the middle of them. Yes, that's the other side of things of course. But even today we can't see a single German aircraft. Admittedly, some small bomber formations flew over us during the night again and must have done some damage to the enemy ships, but we can't detect any visible signs of success.

Through the battery commander's telescope we can see the enemy fleet at the mouth of the Vire. An overwhelming spectacle of the power of the Allies. Ship after ship, funnel after funnel – a sight that absorbs everyone with its sheer military strength. Twenty-seven big freighters each with three or more funnels, ten battleships, twenty or thirty cruisers, hundreds of smaller vessels can be recognised and counted. Really, it looks like a naval review in peacetime. We can clearly see the muzzle flashes from the warships, then the heavy stuff screams overhead and tears deep holes in the marshland. There's nothing we can do except suffer and wait.

Once again, the fighter-bomber formations are approaching the town. They're there, their machines scream into the dive. The dreadful crack of bombs on houses, then dirt and dust are thrown into the air and our tower sways. They turn and come in again. Dammit, get down from this scaffold. My God, that only just missed. But it's no good – we have to climb to the top again as it's the only way we can help our hard-pressed comrades in their battle.

After a long time spent in fruitless observation, during which my howitzer platoon leader asks me three times whether he can open fire, we see some units retreating. At first a few men, individually, then whole groups, platoons coming back at the foot of the mountains. The enemy fire is increasing all the time, but we have no real chance of responding effectively. Then, even more bad luck, a barrel burst. Two men – of course, they're the best gunners – are badly wounded and two others less so. A tragic loss considering how few guns we have for the whole Regiment. Now the rest will be even more hard-pressed.

Meanwhile it has turned into a beautiful day, blue sky, the sun burning hot in the sky. On both sides though, the soldiers continue to suffer. Raiding parties search the city for French vehicles and fuel, and my organisers prove themselves extremely competent once again. A wonderful pale grey limousine rolls up, followed by a little blue one, and we also get our hands on a motorcycle and repair it. At first the Battalion made fun of the Company, but now our transport is the envy of them all.

10.15 hours. Along the single road through the marsh, German troops are working their way towards us, coming under constant artillery fire. Infantry fire can be heard from the direction of our old

6 Parachute Regiment was established in January 1944 on the Wahner Heide by Oberstleutnant Freiherr von der Heydte. At the end of April it was moved to Normandy. Its objective: to defend against enemy airborne landings in the Carentan region. In fact, the Allied invasion began at 0.15 hours on 6 June with extensive airborne landings in the hinterland, before the attck from the sea began at 06.00 hours.

This photograph was taken by Robert Kapa, a war reporter with the first American wave of attackers. The Allied air forces flew 14 674 operations on 6 June and dropped 11 912 bombs. In addition, the invasion of the Allied naval armada was unparalleled: 6 battleships, 122 destroyers, 360 torpedo boats and a couple of hundred frigates, sloops and patrol boats to cover a total of 6480 transport ships, landing craft and special boats. In purely numerical terms, Allied superiority was 10:1.

Thousands of enemy paratroopers were dropped behind the German lines.

For many Americans, the invasion came to an abrupt end in the first minutes. On 'bloody Omaha', the beach between St Laurent and Honorine, the Americans suffered their heaviest casualties.

The Officer Commanding II Parachute Corps, General Meindl, with the Commander of 6 Parachute Regiment, Oberstleutnant von der Heydte (with steel helmet).

Eight men were killed in the crash-landing of this US transport glider type Horsa II.

'The Lion of Carentan', Oberstleutnant Freiherr von der Heydte.

Field Marshal Rommel visits Meindl's II Parachute Corps.

After the fall of Carentan, Generalmajor Ostendorff, Commander of 17 SS Armoured Infantry Division (Panzergrenadier) 'Götz von Berlichingen' is given details of the enemy position by the Commander of 6 Parachute Regiment, Freiherr von der Heydte (in steel helmet).

The American doctor
Thomas Urban Johnson
was taken prisoner by the
Germans that first night,
shortly after the drop on
the command post of
12 Company, III Battalion,
6 Parachute Regiment.
He treated the wounded
of both sides.

...d dressing station of 6 Parachute Regiment in the Carentanregion.

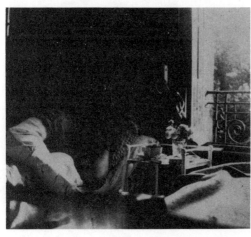

Oberleutnant Pöppel in a military hospital in Paris after being wounded in the arm.

Feldwebel Otto Behne,
leader of Company HQ
personnel in 12 Company.

Obergefreite Herbert Hasenclever
of 12 Company.

Oberjäger Heinz Umland, platoon
HQ personnel leader in 2 platoon.

Oberfeldwebel Alexander Uhlig.

Hauptmann Preikschat,
Battalion Commander I Battalion.

Hauptmann Trebes, Battalion Commander III Battalion.

Regimental HQ as well. Within these few hours, the American breakthrough has made damned good progress.

Now, halfway up the mountain, we can at last see the American infantry units. Well, you fellows, we've been waiting for you for hours. In no time, the order to open fire is given to the howitzer platoon. Shortly afterwards the shooting begins and, after a few corrections, we begin to score direct hits on the Yankees – exactly where we wanted. I lift Doppelstein on my shoulder in sheer joy. Suddenly life on this mountain is fun again as we make the Yankees scatter. How our infantry will celebrate, especially those involved in the rearguard action. It's only a shot in the arm from the rascally artillery, but it brings some relief, especially if we can make every shot count. More groups are working their way to the road. 'Rapid rate of fire'. My poor gunners have had long enough to rest. Their aim is excellent and the range-finder operator is already preparing for new targets.

11.00 hours. Whole columns of infantry appear on the railway line, heading towards us. It's to be hoped that the Americans don't get too far forward, or they'll be able to attack the lads on the flank. To the left and right of the tracks there's marshland, so no alternative route is available to the retreating Germans. Apparently the Americans haven't spotted them yet though, since they aren't directing any artillery fire at the tracks.

Meanwhile the Americans have advanced to the road and our own infantry has reached the protecting bridge in numbers. Now to send over our heavy stuff. Those fellows really do offer a tempting target. Our six-barrelled mortars, which have found the correct range, open up. The shells land right in the middle of the Yankees. The whole area, including our old command post, is now coming under fire from the guns. Our infantry exploits the situation at once and works its way forward at great speed. It's a miracle that the Americans didn't direct their artillery fire at the road and the railway.

The entire Battalion staff has now joined us up here. The Commander and Oberleutnant Ulmer enjoy the spectacle of this less than glorious retreat by our Regimental Commander. Like us, they're also fascinated by the spectacle of the invasion fleet.

Things have quietened down now so I decide to take the chance of visiting the wounded men in my howitzer platoon. My car gets me there in no time, but the men have already been moved. At the station I come across Leutnant Petschke, the Adjutant of I Battalion.

However, he isn't sure what's going on either and knows only that his mob is being almost completely wiped out. The retreating units of II Battalion mill past in long rows, exhausted and staring. The plan was for them to relieve both Battalions, but they had to yield to superior numbers and were lucky not to have been cut off themselves.

In the west the countryside is completely flooded, and it's very boggy in the east as well. The Americans are in the north, and from the south there's only one road leading to us. Since Hauptmann Mager has managed to break through to us with his Battalion, there's no need for Leutnant Degenkolbe to bring them across in shuttle traffic by pneumatic boats. That would have been a really dangerous business. However, all the vehicles and heavy guns have been lost during the march. Now my company is the only one equipped with heavy weapons.

When I return I meet Leutnant Schröder at the church. He's managed to break through to us with a few men from his group. Absolutely exhausted, but still very glad to have made it, the men are sitting down and enjoying their first cigarettes. They've lost some of their uniforms, and they couldn't get most of their weapons over the marsh. We hurry to fetch new gear so that all of them will be fully equipped. Every man is going to be precious in the hours to come, because our losses have certainly been extremely high. According to earlier estimates, the company has lost about five dead and twenty wounded. But not all units were engaged in the fighting i.e. the others had been deployed to less dangerous positions beforehand.

The Inspektors and Hauptfeldwebels are gathering together and our lorries are kept busy fetching supplies from the town. We can't afford to worry about the inhabitants just now – we'll get no supplies of our own so we have to help ourselves. I want to see to the supply train myself. I'm out of cigarettes, too.

At the old Battalion command post I find the Regimental and Battalion staff. The Regimental Commander has arrived with his batmen, dripping wet. Even at this stage, the old fox has managed to trick the enemy. To prevent the enemy fighter-bombers, who were shooting at everything under the sun, from recognising our soldiers, he ordered them to remove their helmets and use them to wave to the aircraft. Up to their knees or bellies in water, they were'nt easy to recognise as German soldiers. Oh yes, our Regimental Commander von der Heydte, he can be a real fox still.

He's borrowed some gear whilst discussing further measures with the Commanders and eating some chicken. Already, he's back in an excellent temper. The Regiment is to try to hold the line at the edge of Carentan until the replacements which have been called for get through. In addition, we are to hold St Come-du-Mont, also 'at all costs'. Regimental HQ will remain here whilst an advance command post is set up at the signal box west of St Come. We are to transfer back to Hill 30 with my old machine-gun and mortar platoons, or what's left of of them.

At the train, stragglers are gathering and waiting to be re-equipped. During ablutions I send orders to my sergeant-major. He's to get together a horse-drawn vehicle with clothing and have it ready to pull out; warm rations to be taken to Hill 30; the entire equipment of the company to be loaded into other such carts still be to be commandeered, so that we'll be able to move quickly even without motor vehicles. The good Sarge is stunned at the host of orders, but it can't be helped. Besides, more supplies have to be organised. Thus excellently refreshed, we travelled back undisturbed. We'll see what else this day has in store for us.

The latest reports say that smaller groups of Americans have been sighted at Cap de Boir, probably part of the remaining airborne landing forces. We can also expect armoured spearheads to attack from the direction of Graignes, as these have crossed the Vire canal in the upper section and are trying to approach Carentan from the south. A race against time begins. The way to Périers will be open to the side which manages to collect its forces to take the defile between the plain and the main highway. The Americans know that as well as we do. Consequently, we're desperately trying to hold Carentan at all costs until our reinforcements get here. On the orders of the Regimental Commander, Oberleutnant von Bethusi (8/6) takes over command with immediate effect. Command post of the 12/6 is established on the northern edge of Hill 30.

Messengers are sent to inform the platoons, which quickly gather on the northern edge and are deployed by Oberfeldwebel Peters according to my instructions. The bulk of the machine-gun platoons are covering the north in such a way that they can also protect Carentan in the centre and also direct fire westwards.

Leutnant Klein's anti-aircraft platoon, previously assigned to the protection of the town, has also been placed under my command. The platoon consists of six 2cm anti-aircraft guns, but not on mobile gun carriages. With their speed and effectiveness, they'll be a great help to us. Two guns are set up on the Hill, two in the valley, the others to protect the Hill. Three mortars, three 12.5cm and three 8cm guns are also put into position on the Hill to the rear of the machine-gun platoons. The command post and observation post are also directly on the Hill, but the telephone central is in its old position.

It takes a massive effort to prepare the new positions for the men and the guns and to establish our observation areas. Since we've acquired an all-too intimate knowledge of the enemy artillery fire, the men are happy to dig their holes. Soon, maybe in the next few hours, we'll have a lot of it to bear.

Late in the night the telephone network is also completed and the important communications ensured. Helbig arrives with a horse-drawn wagon and brings the warm food and excellent coffee we've all been yearning for.

To general satisfaction, it begins to rain gently. The fighting subsides and gives us time to reorganise. The Americans seem to need it too, otherwise they'd certainly have pressed us harder. Enemy artillery fire flares up here and there, but only briefly. Our troops have occupied the edge of the town in front of the marshland and have managed to reorganise themselves.

III Battalion now has to bear the main burden of battle. A Battalion of Russians who have pushed down to us from the north west from the coast, has already been sent to the front. I've put the heavy weapons, twelve machine guns, five 5cm mortars and three 5cm anti-tank guns, as far forward as possible.

Slowly, the front has been stabilised. The men climb tiredly into their holes and fall asleep at once. But for the various commanders, there is no time for sleep yet. For some time, they are busy compiling casualty lists, counting and receiving ammunition and, especially, working out the basic firing distances. After that, even we are allowed to rest a little. It's now 02.00 hours.

9 June. How long have we been asleep? I feel incredibly refreshed, but it was only six hours. It's a beautiful day – and quiet. The sun is golden, the sky is cloudless, there are no sounds of enemy gunfire – it's as though it was peacetime. The night was so quiet that we weren't even woken once. The sentries report a few white signal flares here and there, but nothing else.

The day passes quietly as well. Some reconnaissance patrol activity is reported from both sides, and some firing by the enemy's heavy weapons. Another battery has been assigned to us – 10.5

howitzers. But they have so little ammunition that they can only be used in a real emergency.

We continue to organise ourselves and to drag whatever we can from Carentan. Butter, cheese, real coffee, wine, champagne, socks and shirts – all coveted and needed. The men continue to strengthen the positions, clean their guns and themselves. Ammunition belts are reloaded. 11.00 hours: about twenty Amis can be seen by the old Vire bridges, helping to build footbridges, and there is also considerable activity by supply trucks. Just what our mortars and machine guns have been waiting for. I gladly give permission to open fire, and soon two enemy trucks are in flames. Peters and Domke are the happy marksmen.

An enemy assault gun is moved calmly into position by the church of St Côme-du-Mont, but is removed very quickly after it comes under fire from our positions.

The day passes slowly, with no sign of the attack we had expected from the Americans. Will we get another night of rest? We're also awaiting reinforcements in the form of the outstanding SS Division Götz von Berlichingen. If this is thrown into the battle, with its tanks and guns, its superb equipment and fresh reserves of men, then it might alter the entire situation. But nothing is stirring, and my bad experiences with replacements have made me very pessimistic.

17.00 hours. With Oberleutnant Nade, a plan of action and even – astonishingly – a plan of fire are worked out. The Regiment is reckoning on the Americans crossing the marsh and the river under cover of night. Three barrage fire zones are worked out. Two on the bridges which we so generously allowed to fall intact into the enemy's hands without blowing them up, and the other on the western exit of Carentan. As night is already falling, we have to calculate these zones mathematically.

21.00 hours. On the orders of the Regiment, all the heavy weapons are to aim harassing fire at the two bridges throughout the night. My machine-guns won't reach that far, but apart from them I'm happy to oblige. I've no more worries about ammunition now that I've got the entire reserves of the Regiment's lost heavy weapons at my disposal.

10 June. 00.30 hours. My heavy guns begin their harassing fire on barrage fire zone Berta. But there's nothing to be seen except for the flash of the hits – we can't tell if they're on target. On information received from the infantry, we advance fire by another 200 metres.

My gun lets fly too. The light infantry companies report back to say that the aim is excellent. After I've given further details of the range, I turn in. The rain is pattering gently on the canvas of my tent and soon I'm sunk in a dreamless sleep. That old soldiers' ability to drop off wherever you are and in whatever circumstances has returned after a couple of days in action.

01.00 hours. The telephone rings again to say that on Battalion orders I'm to return to my observation tree, although I had already reported that nothing was happening. I reckon that the Staff has been drinking and has nothing better to do than to deprive its company commanders of their sleep.

Rrriing. Yet again. The Commander! Why am I providing harassing fire with my big gun and not with the machine guns? Crazy question from the Old Man. Because machine gun fire is completely ineffective, as I've already told Oberleutnant Nade, and because the Battalion has ordered me to provide harassing fire with all the guns I can. As a result of telling the truth I get a dreadful dressing down. God – and now this unfortunate gun is firing again, despite the order I've just given to cease fire. Rrring – now there's chaos, the Old Man is back on the line, even more furious with me than before. Now the word is that my mortars are firing too short. But that's not possible, since the firing data has been precisely calculated and checked. As I've been firing for two hours, and accurately at that, then I can't suddenly be firing too short using the same calculations. It's enough to make you puke – the Old Man has suddenly gone crazy.

02.10 hours. Three red Very lights over barrage firing zone Berta! That's the agreed signal of an enemy attack, so I respond with all the guns I have that can reach.

My guns find the range very quickly. Equally quickly the Old Man is on the telephone again. Why am I firing with my big heavy gun again, after he expressly ordered me not to? Because a curtain barrage is the warning sign to the infantry that the enemy is making a major attack, and such a barrage, in general, is only fired when there is danger. But in such a case all heavy guns are to fire, and it's not entirely clear to me why my gun should be the only one to remain silent. But the Regimental Commander is always right – or at least he thinks he is – and I'm removed from my company immediately. His protége Nade, who is actually a fine fellow, is to take over. It's easy to imagine my bitterness. My platoon leaders, who have gone through the whole business with me, are furious as well, but there's nothing to be done. The scum up there always stick together: the

Adjutant naturally sticks by his Commander and won't accept the responsibility for his order.

When I report to him on his orders, it is now 04.00 hours and he's already asleep. Consequently, I don't get the chance to clear my name straight away. As my master has gone to bed, why shouldn't his servant? After informing both Leutnants where I would be, I turn in and sleep – sleep deep into the morning, undisturbed in a soft bed.

Unfortunately I get a bitter awakening, since the Commander has scarcely laid eyes on me before he starts shouting and demanding to know where I've been hiding. I can prove my case through the two Leutnants, since I'd informed them where I'd be. However, one of them wasn't there and the other one simply denied it (that was Leutnant Mundt, the liar). Thank heaven, this storm subsides when I'm able to prove beyond doubt that I'm telling the truth. But the upshot of the whole business is that I, a veteran soldier, am now stuck here with the Commander as ADC no.6, i.e. officer courier.

During the morning, a small number of enemy assault parties manage to reach the bank, but are driven back by our troops. So far the front is holding firm, but it can't be held indefinitely since we have so few heavy weapons. Moreover, we have no real confidence in the infantry we've picked up and the Russian soldiers assigned to us. Everything that's crawling around in the area is collected indiscriminately into battle groups, mainly under the command of Hauptmann Becker, a holder of the German Cross in gold.

That afternoon, the whole sector remains quiet. Only in the evening hours does the infantry report intensified artillery fire, increasing slowly but steadily.

At 18.00 hours there follows the first major attack on our left flank at Pommenauque. The first assault fails, amid heavy enemy casualties. 10 and 11 Companies are in the thick of the fighting. In both of them, clear signs of demoralisation are beginning to appear. Several factors are having their effect: the retreat, the overwhelming superiority of the enemy artillery, and especially the loss of the best leaders (Oberleutnant Wagner was killed on 7 June by a direct hit from the artillery, whilst Oberleutnant Prive died of wounds on the same day at St Côme-du-Mont.)

At 22.00 hours the Americans make a major penetration of our system at Pommenauque. An immediate counterattack led by Oberleutnant Märk fails to break through, and collapses bloodily. Our excellent Battalion doctor, Dr Schad, yet again has his hands full, and our medical personnel perform their usual quiet but selffless duty. Now the Americans are pouring over the marsh road to the northern edge of Carentan.

The Commander of the SS Panzer Division Götz von Berlichingen arrived a short time ago, and he is keen to offer encouragement to our troops in the front line. Yet despite his promise that his tanks will be there in a short time, even he can't save the situation. The men brace themselves one more time, advance again, but are always driven back. Backed by their powerful artillery, the Americans continue to advance, and fog makes any accurate assessment of the situation increasingly difficult. At 22.00 hours the Regimental Commander is forced to give up the position at Carentan. The troops leave their positions and withdraw, in what is more of a flight than an orderly retreat. To our great good fortune, this happens without the Americans realising what's happening and pressing after us. Even Hill 30, so crucial to our defence and with Oberleutnant Nade now in control, can no longer be held.

If we were in Carentan itself something might still have been done, but we've been forced into the hedgerows and no longer have the marsh ahead of us to protect us. We'd certainly be extremely vulnerable to an attack. The new line, reconnoitred some hours ago, lies along the line St Georges be Bohon – Saintenny – La Moisentrie – Blehou. The line is occupied at 23.00 hours, without any enemy pressure, and the commanders immediately make minor alterations to the positions. During the night, rough-and-ready protections are erected against artillery bombardment. The arrival of the SS Regimental Commander has made all of us more confident. At dawn by the latest, the advance parties of the Division will be arriving. So the night passes quietly, with hardly any shooting at all.

11 June. In the first hours of the morning I travel by motor cycle, on the orders of the Regimental Commander, to the Corps staff at St Lo. My instructions:

1. Situation report.
2. Request of the Regiment to be placed under the command of the SS Panzer Division, as no orders at all are coming in from 91 Infantry Division and the SS Division is nearest to us.
3. Provision of supply.

The weather is grey and cloudy as I roar off on my motor-cycle, so at least we'll be less harassed by enemy aircraft. I reach St Lo without incident. After some delay, we locate the Corps Staff in an old seminary, a big, strong building. Life here is lived almost entirely underground. The staff is accommodated in a very deep, complex bunker built by the army engineers. There are at least twenty steps down into it and light is provided by an underground power source.

Soon I'm standing in front of the senior staff officer, GSO 1 (ops). To my pleasure, the Colonel tells me that the Regiment has been mentioned in the Wehrmacht Report, and sends his congratulations to our Regimental Commander. He says that the whole Corps is extremely impressed by the performance of the Regiment. (They haven't understood how badly we were led.) General Marx is pleased as well, and also agrees to our various requests. Everything is settled to our benefit.

I'm also able to pinch a stack of maps, so vital for us. Having accomplished my mission, I roar back to base. Shot-up and burned-out vehicles are littering the road like mile-posts. Burned trucks, shot to pieces by fighter-bombers, are everywhere. There are hardly any other vehicles moving on the roads. We reach our command post at Blehou without incident.

Meanwhile, the first Battalion of the SS Division has arrived and its officers are attending a situation discussion with the Commander. All first-class fellows, a superb officer corps, like ours used to be in the early years. The Divisional Commander, a holder of the Knight's Cross, makes a particularly good impression. All his officers are devoted to him. The Battalion Commanders are excellent too, and include two more holders of the Knight's Cross. The Artillery Commander, a schoolmaster in peacetime, is a likeable old fellow who wins us all over at once.

The Battalion is moved into the line immediately. Most important, it is to hold the dangerous right sector, which stretches over the main Carentan-Périers road as far as the runway. In the early morning, the Forward Observation Officers of the SS Artillery rush ahead to work out their firing data. In the evening, there's another discussion here concerning our planned counterattack on Carentan. Officers pore over tables and maps, making enthusiastic calculations. Warning orders to resupply with ammunition have already been sent out to all units.

At 22.00 hours the following warning order is issued:

1. The Götz von Berlichingen Division, supported by 6 Parachute Regiment, to attack Carentan in the counterattack on 12 June 1944.
2. Start of attack at X hour.
3. Boundary for the attacking Battalions: main Carentan-Périers road. a) 12/6 (which already knows the terrain) with two SS

platoons to strengthen the right side of the main road. b) I./SS Regiment 37 on the left. c) left support II./Regiment 6 under the command of Hauptmann Mager.
4. Objective of the SS Battalion: to break through to the northern edge of Carentan. Objective of the III./6: a controlled advance up to the railway line with the right flank in touch with the SS.
5. Attack to be supported by SS Artillery Regiment G.v.B. and two SS assault gun batteries.
6. In the event of good progress, the Division intends to break through to St Côme-du-Mont and to establish a bridgehead there.
Signed: Ossendorf, SS Divisional Commander

This order is received with immense pleasure by the troops. They reckon that we'll be advancing again now, back to Carentan, scene of so much earlier fighting. My men are particularly happy to be going back to Hill 30. Many of our dead comrades lie there, left unburied, as well as our weapons and especially our 2cm guns. Perhaps we'll even manage to get them back intact by making a surprise attack, they think.

On the other hand, us 'Old Men' at headquarters are rather less optimistic. Hauptmann Peisser, like me, thinks the situation is far from rosy, since we have so few men to deploy. We don't even dare think about a breakthrough to St Côme-du-Mont. Against the enemy, we haven't been given adequate forces. It's incomprehensible to us why an entire SS Regiment hasn't been deployed instead of one miserable Battalion. It's doubtful whether adequate support will be provided from the heavy weapons, because the Artillery Commander himself has expressed reservations about whether he'll have received adequate supplies of ammunition in time. The whole thing seems to be a highly doubtful business, and it seems very unlikely that we'll be able to force home our attack. The SS think they can do it easily, they've arrived with enormous idealism – but they'll get the surprise of their lives against this enemy, which is not short of skill itself.

12 June. 05.00 hours. The night has passed peacefully with only the usual light signals to disturb us. Now we're waiting for our artillery to begin the preparation. Everywhere there's an atmosphere of feverish excitement and expectancy. Will our troops manage to drive the enemy back?

Our artillery' fire begins tentatively, but gradually increases in intensity. However, the enemy isn't asleep either, and is shelling our positions with harassing fire. The noise of battle is useful for our advancing assault guns, providing 'noise camouflage'. On the roads and access routes, in the meadows and fields, SS men and paratroopers are waiting for the order to advance. The minefield lanes have already been cleared secretly during the night. 'X-Hour' has been set for 06.00 hours.

Now the time has come. The artillery has been keeping up a heavy barrage for 15 minutes, the assault guns have been moved forward to the furthest point where the hedgerows offer cover. At the stroke of 06.00 hours our artillery fire creates a fire-screen above the positions to be attacked. Simultaneously the tanks advance, accompanied by the infantry. The enemy line has already been reached, with hardly any shots being fired from there.

My men are fairly well acquainted with the terrain and move towards the old line. Widely spaced and in echelon, they advance from hedge to hedge. As they approach their objective, they come under semi-automatic fire. A sniper in a tree! A burly lance-corporal, a Bavarian or Tyrolean with a neat moustache, brings two men down from the trees single-handedly but is then hit and killed. Two others are wounded. This much we can see from the observation post. Then we gather round the radio equipment to hear the incoming reports and get the details of the situation.

07.30 hours. Report from SS Battalion I/37: Advancing steadily despite very stiff enemy resistance. Americans moving to the north. Enemy groups still situated between our spearheads. Own casualties moderately high.

09.00 hours. Report from the left flank: Have reached outskirts of Carentan, strong enemy groups still in rear. Request artillery fire on Carentan since noise of tanks detectable there.

09.15 hours. Report from the right flank: Unable to prevail against strong resistance without tanks. Approximately 500 metres territory gained by 09.00 hours.

09.50 hours. Report from SS Battalion I/37: Attack at a standstill in front of Carentan. Enemy attacking from Carentan with tanks.

10.45 hours. Forced to withdraw under massive enemy pressure.

Then everything happens with lightning speed. The Commander of the SS troops has realised that only our own position can now be held, and orders a rapid withdrawal to the initial position.

The troops are pouring back, but can still be intercepted and made to reinforce the line of defence. Then the Americans rush forward, but at least they've given us enough time to gather. They must surely have reckoned it was a trick and not had sufficient confidence to advance so fast, otherwise things would have been damned difficult for us.

So the counterattack has failed, just as we had thought it must. No breakthrough to St Côme-du-Mont. Our casualties are very high, particularly in the SS Battalion and on our left flank. My company has also suffered considerably. Its estimate, yet to be confirmed, is of the following losses:

> Killed: 3 Feldwebel, 2 Oberjäger, 5 men
> Wounded: 3 Oberjäger, 23 men
> Missing: 1 Oberjäger, 5 men

Yet again, it's generally the best men who have been lost. Especially tragic is the loss of our two machine gun Unteroffizier, Domke and Runge, the best in the Company. And we've had to leave the badly wounded men in the hands of the enemy since we couldn't take them with us during the retreat.

Now it's all quiet on the battlefield. Here and there people are working to restore order. The lorries are moving ceaselessly to evacuate the wounded, ammunition is being replaced, and most important of all, the units are being reorganised. The III SS Battalion 37 has to be brought in because I Battalion's casualties are simply too high. Our units, which were fighting on the right flank, return to us and our Battalion thus takes over a sector again. The companies are deployed as follows: On the right, 12 Company rifle platoon under Leutnant Schroeder, then 9 Company in the strength of a reinforced platoon under Feldwebel Mauth. 10 Company, a platoon under Fahnenjunker-Feldwebel Hupe. 11 Company, still the strongest with three platoons under Oberleutnant Märk, apart from myself the only remaining company commander in the Battalion. Battalion command post by the bend in the road outside Meautie. I'm returning to my Company as well, since Oberleutnant Nade is being assigned elsewhere.

The Company now consists of a machine gun section with two heavy machine guns led by Fahnenjunker-Unteroffizier Binder, one heavy mortar section with three 8cm mortars under Feldwebel Ohm and Oberfeldwebel Rentsch, two rifle platoons under Leutnant Schröder and Oberfeldwebel Rentsch. A pitiful remnant of a company which was once so proud and strong. I've got so many platoon leaders that I don't know what to do with them. We're short of weapons, or else we could set up new platoons. But that's what's happened to almost all the companies, although they have it much easier than the heavy weapons companies.

The Commander is keeping me near him now. It's the old, old story – eventually you're bound to get behind the lines with the Staff; heavy weapons can be directed most effectively from the command post, because the Commander receives his reports and always has particular requests to make of the commander of the heavy weapons as a result.

In the course of the afternoon we manage the redeployment without being disturbed by the enemy. Now the men are feverishly digging earthworks. It will probably be only a matter of hours until the Americans attack.

Evening comes, then the night, but nothing happens.

13 June. The weather has cleared up again, and the enemy air activity intensifies. No vehicle on the road is safe from the fighter-bombers and Lightnings. It's become virtually impossible to travel the roads by day, but we've already prepared for this. Enemy air activity is at its height in the morning, midday and evening hours, so these hours are avoided. Anti-aircraft lookouts are assigned to each vehicle, so that whenever enemy aircraft approach they can be driven into cover. But despite all these precautionary measures, the pilots are always finding new victims. This morning, as my batman is bringing my wonderful pale grey limousine back to the train, the car is shot up on the Carentan-Périers road. Fortunately my batman escapes, suffering only from shock. The day ends with the harassing fire from the enemy that we've all grown used to. No casualties.

14 June. Moderate artillery fire from the enemy and ourselves. I use this relatively peaceful day to check on the train. Everywhere animals are being slaughtered and seized. Naturally enough, good food raises the men's courage for the fight. The old saying is true – an army marches on its stomach.

16 June. The usual artillery fire. The weather has become summery and warm.

17 June. Since the early hours of the morning there has been increased fire along the Battalion's entire sector. Almost every company has suffered casualties. More than five men have been wounded in my own company. Are the Americans going to attack today? They've certainly given us enough breathing-space. In the wider picture, Cherbourg fortress is in the centre of the fighting and is being attacked by the enemy with all his forces, which has been a very great relief for us. Will it be our turn now? It almost looks that

way, because the artillery fire is constantly increasing. And yet the expected attack hasn't materialised. The night is wild and we spend it on a drinking session with the SS as our guests. The situation is discussed frankly and it becomes clear that the SS is in a position to make an objective judgement. If we haven't managed to drive the enemy back at all after ten days' fighting, how on earth are we ever going to get them out? The transportation of our SS and armoured units is taking a very long time, given the constant bombardment of the routes. Meanwhile the enemy has had time to land more troops and equipment, to consolidate his position. Although a few ships have been sunk, they are of little significance given the extent of Allied power. In these circumstances, we are not very optimistic. Almost all of us are convinced that unless we succeed in driving the enemy out within three weeks at most, then we will have lost the war. The theme of invasion has become the story of our lives, and dominates the conversation during these evenings.

18 June. Nothing of significance to report.

19 June. the usual. The enemy artillery fire doesn't affect those men who are safely in their dug-outs, but it still finds victims every day and thus slowly but surely saps the strength of the Battalion.

20 June. Waiting – waiting – waiting.

21 June. Generally, our own recce patrols are sent out under cover of darkness. The men spend hours lying in front of enemy lines, trying to find out more information, usually without success. The SS have also sent out night-time assault parties and brought back prisoners, which are really valuable for us. But even here our Regimental Commander does not stick to his own first principles of reconnaissance instruction.

22 June. Excellent progress is being made on the consolidation of our positions. The individual holes are now connected by trenches to create a unified line, and well-disguised observation holes have been driven through the earth walls. The roads have already been mined, and each night our engineers are at work mining the land in front of our positions. Barbed wire, prepared by our supply men, is also being put into position.

Each day that passes enables us to strengthen our position, althouogh we still have a lot to do. From bitter experience we know never to stop the work of consolidation and improvement, but to carry on until the last possible moment.

23 June. To our delight we've obtained a heavy gun again, the only one in the Battalion. My howitzer platoon leader Doppelstein is

especially pleased and is already busy organising and assembling the platoon. For the last few days he has been acting as ADC with the Battalion. By evening we are ready. Tomorrow, we'll be waiting for action. Let's just see how this brand-new cannon can shoot. We've also been provided with two 8cm mortars, which we immediately prepare for action. Now all we're lacking are the heavy machine-guns all the men are desperate to get their hands on.

24 June. For two days, three men from 11 Company have been lying just in front of the enemy lines trying to discover suitable opportunities for a night-time combat patrol. Needless to say, they get a great deal of fun out of it. Now that the enemy has left us in peace for so long the men have rediscovered their composure and are in good spirits.

Today we discover that the neighbouring Battalion had a success yesterday. A combat patrol of twelve men, which had already penetrated the enemy trenches once before, went over again last night and blew up six American heavy mortars without suffering any losses themselves. Much envy in our Battalion, of course.

In the evening an American scout car races towards our lines along the mined road, but is captured by the Battalion. It's the same type that I'm already acquainted with from Sicily – a nice little car with a .50 calibre machine gun mounted on it. However, we soon remove the gun to allow us to steer the car better, and also because of the shortage of ammunition.

These days have contained some pleasant surprises, but it soon begins to get boring. The daily tour of the positions takes two hours, then I'm more or less unemployed for the rest of the day.

For the first time since this fighting began, we get post today. Great joy, of course, for all the lucky recipients in their bunkers and foxholes. A little bit of home in this miserable existence.

Like the others, today passes without any major enemy activity, except that the artillery fire is increasing all the time. In particular, all the men fear surprise mortar attacks, since you don't hear the gun being discharged and therefore don't get the chance to take cover in time. A sudden hit – which leaves some more men lying on their bellies.

25 June. The men from the Staff are working day and night on the bunker I proposed. A hole two and a half metres deep has already been dug in the earth, where it splits into two passages, both descending deeper into the earth. At night we can hear the monotonous noise of the Russians shovelling, since we have involved

them in the work as well. The bunker is already very large, and in two or three days we'll all have shelter from the heavy artillery and the bombs.

08.30 hours. We're at our morning ablutions, still undertaken with great ceremony, when a number of aircraft suddenly approach. And to our utter astonishment, they are German fighters, and 12 of them. Amazing – that's the first we've seen since this fighting began. In wide echelon and flying very low, they roar over the trees and hedges. then we hear the sound of the aircraft guns and machine guns, obviously directed at enemy vehicles on the road. Now at least the Yanks will know how it feels to come under fire from above.

The American Thunderbolts almost wiped me out today. As I was driving back from a visit to the train, the anti-aircraft lookout shouted 'aircraft'. I just had time to slow down and turn into a side road flanked by tall poplars. In the nick of time – the aircraft roared overhead, but he couldn't discover where we were hidden and flew off. My men admitted to me that they were damned scared then, not so much by the aircraft, as by my driving when I careered off the main road. But I was lucky after all, and it seems that I'm getting myself a reputation for it. That apart, nothing is happening. We drink fizz from dawn till dusk and clown around.

26 June. Today the first Iron Crosses and Infantry Assault Badges are given to the Battalion, handed out at 13.00 hours. The men fall in in front of the Regimental Commander, who takes it on himself to make the first award personally. The eyes of the young soldiers light up when the Iron Cross is pinned on their chests in recognition of their courageous service. That old warhorse Feldwebel Mauth is awarded the Iron Cross First Class – he deserves it.

Others of my mob get the Iron Cross Second Class, among them the excellent range-finder operator from Company headquarters, Unteroffizier Feltes, and our Company lout Herbert Hasenclever, an impossible character but a good soldier. Kurt Franz, a veteran with the Iron Cross First Class like myself, comes away empty-handed. There was nothing else for us.

Our underground bunker is now being shored up and improved. It's already given us good protection on a couple of occasions when the shells were raining down. We've already had to provide a new toilet because the old one came under fire too often. What on earth could we have written to a grieving mother if her son was killed whilst sitting on the bog?

22.15 hours. The Americans make an attack by night – perhaps one platoon in strength. It is beaten off in front of 9 Company's positions. Dead bodies are left lying on the ground, but one badly injured man is brought in. It turns out to be an English paratrooper, not a Yank. This proves that it isn't just the original enemy troops who are facing us now. He dies during the night without us managing to get any important information out of him. These blokes are well-trained, and respond to every question with the comment 'I can't tell you'.

27 June. According to Divisional reports, the situation at St Lo is becoming increasingly critical. If this front falls back, our position here would become indefensible as well. The entire left flank would then be left completely exposed.

An assault party by 11 Company is planned for tonight. To get better fire discipline I fetch up my tried and tested mortar platoon leader, Feldwebel Ohm, from the train. He responds with commendable enthusiasm, even though he's still limping and having to use a stick.

23.00 hours. It's raining softly on the leaves and branches, which is a great advantage for the business in hand since it provides a natural sound camouflage. The final preparations have been made, the Company Commander reports to the Commander, who's been drinking again, that all is ready. The assault party, consisting of an Oberjäger and ten men, has already crept softly forwards and is now within reach of the combat outposts. We're just waiting for the green signal flare to tell us to fire our mortars and enable the squad to make the final push.

00.45 hours. Green signal flare!

Immediately, our mortars start firing in quick succession. Everything goes off without a hitch! The assault party runs forward, reaches its objective, sends up a white signal. At that moment, our mortars start to fire further forwards and provide a sustained barrage of fire on the area of penetration.

From over there – nothing. Not a shot – nothing.

I order the men to cease fire, but to remain ready for action.

02.30 hours. Report from the leader of the assault party that these enemy positions, long observed, have been abandoned.

On the order of the Commander, the assault party is to remain in the enemy position with a few men and a telephone, to observe events next day.

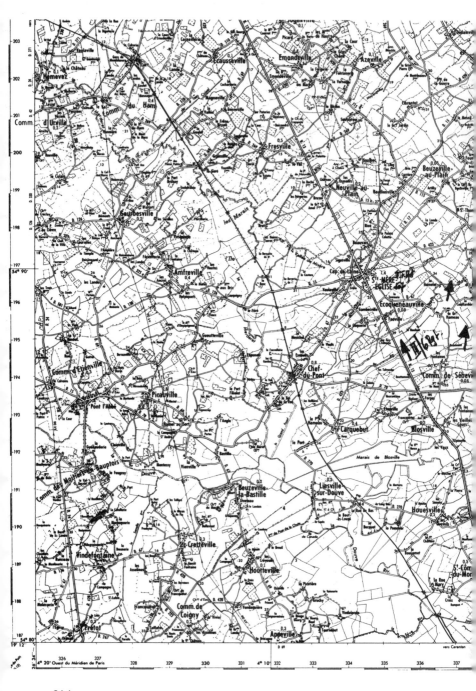

214

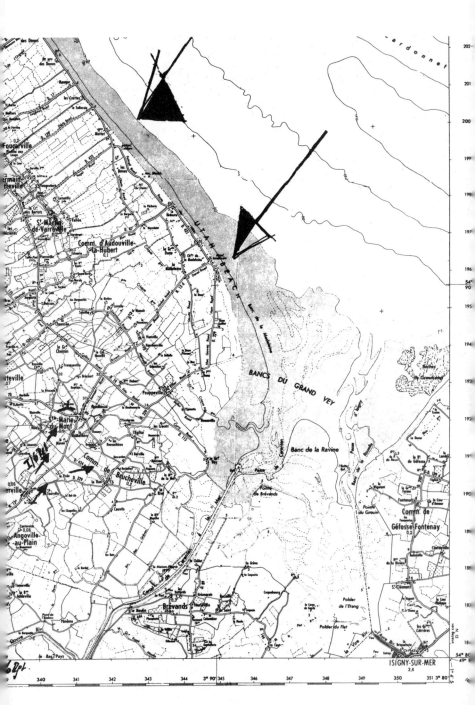

The enemy has apparently recovered from the shock and is sending over a continuous barrage in revenge for our assault. But too late – we're all safely back in our dug-outs.

28 June. Whispered reports from our 'eavesdroppers', but of no importance. Nothing happens.

I travel to the rear in that nippy little car again to clean myself up properly. The Regiment has set up a delousing station and steam bath at the advanced field dressing station and it's available for our use. A wonderful feeling to let that hot water trickle down one's body. There is also some decent food available at the train. Coutances, which we visit briefly, has been almost completely destroyed. We clamber over the high piles of ruined buildings, looking for undamaged objects we might be able to use. Above all, we take entrenching tools with us. Our little car is loaded down when we drive back. At the front, nothing much has happened. Apart from the usual harassing fire, the enemy hasn't done anything to disturb us.

29 June. No events of note.

30 June. As the month draws to its close, the Yanks make a major attack on the left flank of III./SS Battalion 37 in the early hours of the morning. It fails, due to the resolute resistance of these young soldiers.

At 04.30 hours a fearful artillery bombardment begins which reaches us as well. We're sure that the expected major offensive is about to take place, but in fact it proves to be no more than an operation to obtain better points of departure for the enemy. The manoeuvre fails, which does a great deal to lift the self-confidence of the men.

Tonight we recall our assault party. They bring back interesting sketches and maps of the enemy trench system. These reveal that the Americans are keeping only a few men in their forward lines during the day, but are reinforcing them strongly at night.

For the second time, decorations are awarded. They include close combat clasps for us old hands. As usual, the night passes with drinking and clowning until almost dawn, when the main danger has actually passed.

1 July. Today we hope to occupy ourselves by destroying that damned church tower in Meautie. It affords an excellent view of our positions and it would be a miracle if it wasn't occupied by the enemy.

During a sudden concentration of fire, sustained for five minutes by our artillery, a 'bumblebee' – a 10.5 self-propelled medium field howitzer – is moved forward to an open firing position. It soon scores a direct hit on the church tower, but the thing has thick walls. Eighteen shots are fired at it, there are holes all over the tower and the nave, but it won't fall down. The Battery Commander eventually ceases fire. Five minutes pass, then a hail of fire is directed at us which drives us under cover in our bunker as quickly as possible. The bunker comes under enormous pressure from the weight of the hits, but all that happens is some sand trickling from the walls. The bunker stands as firm as iron.

Doppelstein is desperate to have another try at the tower tomorrow, using our big gun. Perhaps that will bring it down.

We ask our recce patrol, which already knows the terrain in front of 11 Company, to take over a card to the Yanks today. I'm already working on the draft. A white card 30/20cm, with this written on it in English in capital letters:

Invitation

We cordially invite the American Commander with his staff to a variety show on 6 July, and request his presence. The variety is entitled: Parisian Women.

Much amusement from everyone who sees it, especially at the picture of naked French women. The patrol takes it forward under cover and fixes it to a stick. The Americans will scarcely be able to believe their eyes when they see our little joke.

2 July. The placard, which was taken over during the night, is clearly visible to us. The Americans must have been able to read it with the naked eye.

In the early hours of the morning our cannon is brought forward. The firing distances are soon worked out and the gun is ready to fire. We've moved it forward to improve our chances of success as it's naturally more effective over shorter distances. The gun is incredibly light, so there will be no difficulty in moving it back in the event of enemy fire. The platoon leader reports that they are ready for action, and I give permission to open fire. The first shot is too high, but the very next one tears a beautiful hole in the tower. Eight shots, each better than the one before, but the monster just won't fall. At any rate we've made it extremely difficult for any observer to work up there.

Our various observation posts report enemy activity throughout the morning. Groups of men, often small groups, are moving about over there, though not in the most vulnerable spots only 90 metres away from us. On several occasions Binder, my best marksman, manages to hit enemy soldiers. After that, the others are more careful.

During my tour of the positions our fellows take great care and put 5cm shells in front of my nose for 200 metres as covering fire! Every couple of metres Oberleutant Seibert and I have to fall flat on our faces, but I'm not angry with Seibert for crawling round me all the time. Although he's fairly scrawny he can still ward off a few splinters, and if he enjoys protecting my valuable life, why not? He's a good fellow, but still inexperienced.

It's now possible to cross almost the whole of the Battalion's sector in the trenches. Despite the constant harrassing fire, the men have done a thoroughly respectable job. The trenches are as high as a man and fitted with small entrances. At least a metre layer of wood and earth, whilst screens of timber and brushwood have been erected on the exposed sections. The anti-tank gun in the defile has been installed and camouflaged carefully. Over the past 14 days, the whole area has been transformed.

3 July. The weather is still warm and beautiful. Most of the men are sitting in front of their dug-outs to enjoy the sun. Weapons are being cleaned, gear kept in good order. A sudden concentration of fire from the enemy, but it lands behind our lines. And why not – why shouldn't they get their share of our daily torment back there? Once again groups are observed on the other side today, arriving with instructions. Are they meant as a relief or for an attack? In the evening we are again visited by our old friend from the SS engineers, a Sturmführer from Upper Silesia. So there's a special wine brought out. When Hauptmann Mager arrives as well, it's clear that there has to be a celebration.

4 July. Midnight has passed long since, but only a few of our guests have left. The carousing goes on and on, although at least it's no longer quite so loud.

It's about 04.00 hours when a particularly powerful concentration of fire from the enemy artillery drives us underground. A sustained barrage rolls overhead – according to the report, most of it is hitting our most advanced positions occupied by II Battalion and the artillery positions. Soon almost all lines have been broken and the maintenance men have to set off on their dangerous missions. I advise the guests to return to their posts, since the fire has now lasted for over half an hour, and its intensity is increasing. Although the Commander laughs incredulously, the guests leave.

05.30 hours. Three signal flares illuminate the sky before it is fully light. The long awaited attack has begun. There's screening smoke over our positions, the enemy artillery fire gradually moves to the rear. That damned aircraft, the artillery observer, is working overhead, but our weapons can't reach it. Our mortars have already been deployed in the endangered sector and are hard at work. Motor cycles race to our own artillery units because the telephone lines have all been broken, of course. The Americans are lucky to have their practical equipment, their walkie-talkies.

The radio operators key and encode, everything at fever pitch, it's now down to each individual to see that our defence is successful. Meanwhile my batman prepares my old light equipment pack. Nearby, in moments snatched between all the incoming reports, people are drinking genuine, strong coffee and managing to eat a few mouthfuls of food.

06.15 hours. The first significant enemy penetration has just been reported on the boundary beween our Battalion and II Battalion. Although 11 Company begins an immediate counterattack, it fails to recover the ground lost.

I suggest to the Commander that I should be allowed to make a counter-attack with my reserve platoon, and I've already put on my steel helmet in order to make my way to the men. It doesn't take long to organise the platoon. After a short summary of the situation, we move forwards carefully but steadily. A mortar attack forces us to take cover for a few minutes. Then we reach an old sunken road, just in front of the old main line of defence. Dead Americans are lying all around, items of equipment are all over the ground. I set guards on all sides. Shells are landing all round us, damned close, but we manage to find effective cover between two bales of straw. I send a messenger back to report that I have reached a sunken road without encountering the enemy, and to request the advance of a second group from the direction of the command post.

Shells fly over again. Then I send one of my men over the sunken road to give cover on the other side, bullets whipping past him as he goes. Unfortunately he can't determine the exact location of the enemy. My batman crosses over as well. Once again, bullets fly past him, but the fellows don't care about that.

Further over the road we can see groups of soldiers. On closer examination they turn out to be our own side. I send one man to make contact and discover their objectives.

Just when I've decided to move further forward, my batman signs to me to be quiet from across the sunken road. Has he heard voices speaking in English? Yes indeed – several of them, coming closer. I quickly pass on the message to my men, get my hand grenades ready and try to creep further forwards. I hear running footsteps – get quickly up onto my knees in time to see an American charging towards us with his gun ready to fire. I snatch up by sub-machine gun and shoot in one rapid movement. He collapses, falling forwards.

I stand up quickly in order to get a better field of fire, but just in time to see another American through the gap. I turn like lightning and raise my sub-machine gun. Then we open fire on each other. I'm hit in the arm – he got me. Damn it, but at least the American has gone down as well. I let myself drop into a hole and listen. My arm hurts like hell.

Outside there is increased noise of battle, especially hand grenades and machine guns. Then things gradually get quieter. I wait half an hour, until the noise has stopped. What has been happening? Have my men has to retreat? Am I alone here? In any event I've got my pistol in my sound left hand so that I can defend myself to the death. According to our reports, American war surgery is like the French – very quick to amputate if cases look doubtful, and even more so where prisoners are concerned. I've cut my right sleeve and seen a huge entry wound just above the elbow. Can only hope there's not too much damage done.

Then I hear men speaking. I can tell they are our men – then I recognise the voice of Oberfeldwebel Rentsch. I call out to them and they get me out of the hole, since I couldn't have done it without help. Rentsch is continuing to advance so I don't want to be in his way. My batman brings me back to the field dressing station and informs the Commander.

Eventually the Hauptmann appears with Oberleutnant Ulmer, tells me I'll be back in five days and gives me cigarettes. This time he'll surely be awarding me the German Cross in Gold – wonder what he'd think if he knew that I don't care about medals any more. Next I'm taken to the casualty clearing station, where the doctors are mainly from the SS. Reserve troops are leaving for the front, but for me personally there'll be no more fighting for some time.

I have my first operation in St Martin, then travel as far as Rennes to the base hospital. After another operation I'm sent to Le Mans three weeks later, and finally to the base hospital in Paris, and excellent modern hospital. Apart from my 'Stuka', my outstretched arm, there is nothing wrong with me, so I begin to flirt enthusiastically with an attractive French nurse. She is really nice, but unfortunately no more than nice.

In the hospital we hear about the attempt to assassinate the Führer. Although there are SS officers here as well, we all discuss things quite openly. The are front-line soldiers the same as us, not the Black SS or the 'golden pheasants', which is what we call the party bigwigs who run around behind the lines. Even the SS men reckon that if we manage to win the war, the party will have to be dealt with afterwards. Most of them don't agree with the assassination attempt, but the prevailing opinion is that the Generals are at fault for relinquishing their famed leadership qualities to the so-called 'Greatest Military Leader of all Time'. How did the poor buggers at the front, and the exhausted civilian population at home, deserve to be led so badly? We have many anxious questions about the future and our prospects in this long war. Even the most confident among us have doubts. And now the 'German Greeting', the Nazi salute, has been introduced to replace the traditional military salute. It has been made quite clear to everyone who is in charge. No – the wounded are most definitely not happy.

Soon I'm travelling home to Germany on the hospital train, to bombed, exhausted battered Germany. Over emergency bridges, through ruined towns, constantly being stopped by air raids and track repairs. No cheerful waves like there were two years ago, just an almost mechanical and resigned lift of the arm as we pass. It makes us thoroughly depressed. I spend a few days in Kulmbach military hospital and am then transferred as an ambulant to the Luftwaffe hospital in Munich. Here, as a representative of my Regiment, I am awarded th Close Combat Clasp in Silver and the Wound Badge in Silver. Frankly I could just as easily have done without them, and in any case the only decoration I wear on my uniform is my Iron Cross First Class. But I'm home again, and for a few weeks at least that's the most important thing. My parents, my sister and friends all mollycoddle me enormously. But my fiancée, in Magdeburg, can't get permission to travel. War work is the reason. Painful, but understandable. Kurt Schlegel, a friend of my old pal Friedl Überreither who was to become my old good friend, got maried during these weeks and we travelled to Chiemsee to celebrate. Wedding night in Heuschober – something to be glad about, at any rate.

From our Munich suburb of Ottobrunn, about 12 kilometres away from the Marienplatz in the city centre as the crow flies, we can see the bomber formations dropping their cargo of fire and death over Munich in the blazing sunshine. It's a damned shame. We leave each other depressed, thinking not just of those poor people there, but everywhere. Almost every night, and now by day as well, hurrying to the bunkers with a few personal belongings, suffering the terrible explosions, the infernal noise all around, the trembling, waiting for death at any moment. Aren't the old men, the women and children the real heroes? And they can't even open their mouths to cry out in fear, in case the air raid warden is still a committed Nazi who might report them. No, it's better by far to be out there, back at the front.

Retreat in the West, 1944

My Regimental Commander, Oberstleutnant von der Heydte, wrote to me on 3 September 1944:

On the basis of the instruction from the Paratroop AOK 11/ Adjutant no. 4869/44 of 13.8.44, after your discharge from the military hospital you are assigned once again to 6 Parachute Regiment. I am happy to be able to give you this information and hope that you will soon be recovered. I also ask you to inform me when your recovery can be expected. All the men are glad to know that you will be leading them again and are waiting impatiently for your return.

I greet you in old comradeship . . .

None of the entreaties of my fiancée, my parents, brothers and sisters, friends had any effect. My arm was still in a sling, but I had to get back to the Front, to my dearly-won 12 Company. I couldn't bear to sit around listening to any more defeatist speeches (although I was slowly but surely being affected by them as well), when I knew what my comrades were going through. I had to get back to the Regiment.

At first I travelled to Aschersleben or Oschersleben, I'm not sure which because I haven't any notes. Either I no longer had the desire to write them or, more likely, these last months had just been too hectic. I vaguely remember one time in the mess when the garrison commander, an Oberst who was a veteran of the First World War, mentioned that he had recently been at the Führer's headquarters and that a 'miracle weapon' was going to be introduced soon. I couldn't stop myself commenting that the situation at the Front was so appalling because of the shortage of vehicles and heavy artillery, and particularly because of the absence of any kind of air support. If we had these, we wouldn't need any 'miracle weapons'. This wasn't just my own opinion. It was shared by other line officers. However, I soon found out that I was being accused of defeatist attitudes because of it.

By the middle of November I was on my way. After an exhausting train journey, interrupted on numerous occasions by air raids, I reached the Parachute Service School near Arnheim, but on the German side of the border. The newly established Assault Battalion of the Parachute Army was also in training here. I was assigned to Hauptmann von Hütz, holder of the Knight's Cross, as an instructor in heavy weapons. However, this experience only lasted a few days. More or less overnight, we heard that all the experienced, battle-tried officers would be transferred to the von der Heydte battle group, which days later was to be almost completely wiped out or captured after a drop during the Ardennes offensive. Since my arm was still damaged, I wasn't permitted to go with them. Well, a few months ago nothing could have stopped me from making the jump, but nowadays I wasn't so whole-hearted about it. When I did return to the unit, Commander von der Heydte welcomed me gladly, but then spoke to me very seriously: 'Herr Pöppel, be careful, I've already had a report on your defeatist opinions at the replacement training regiment.' We had reached the stage when a line officer could not speak his opinion even within his own circle, among comrades, without a Nazi officer reporting it. That hurt, and only the pleasure with which my comrades welcomed me back did something to ease the pain.

After the transfer of the best men to the battle group, the Training School was disbanded and I was assigned as Company Commander to 4th Company of the Assault Battalion under Hauptmann Eduard Hübner. Plenty of new faces here, and only a few veteran paratroopers. Pleasant, bespectacled Leutnant Giffelt was adjutant, Temporary Company Commander was Leutnant Joswig, and Becker and Stephan were Oberleutnants. We didn't get much time to rest. In January 1945 we were moved to Winterswijk in Holland and thrown into the battleground around Roermond and Venlo. Then there were a few quiet days. The Americans managed to capture Aachen, but not to cross the Roer – we held them up there.

The river was usually shrouded in mist, especially in the mornings. As as result, we managed to send recce patrols over in pneumatic boats, bring back prisoners and discover details of the enemy units. Our rations were still good, so we gave many loaves of bread to the local people. A lot of Dutch girls hung on to us, went with us, and were to regret it bitterly later on. As far as possible, I talked to these girls and tried to convince them not to. You could already see what would happen.

Retreat in the West 1944

American infantry advancing in the Reichswald at Xanten. By far the biggest contingent of German paratroopers was concentrated between the Rhine and the Maas. In the battle for the Reichswald alone, four Paratroop Divisions took part. Looking back on this battle, Field Marshal Montgomery gave his own assessment: 'Never in the course of the whole war had enemy units achieved such bitter resistance as the paratroopers in the battle for the Rhineland.'

Retreat from the Reichswald through the shattered town of Xanten.

AUFRUF

an die männliche Bevölkerung der Stadt Venlo!

Sämtliche männliche Einwohner der Stadt VENLO im Alter van 18-50 Jahren haben sich am 21.12.1944, um 14.00 Uhr mit Schanzzeuch (Spaten, Hacken und Schaufeln) bei dem Kampfkommandant der Stadt Venlo, Bürgemeister van Rijnsingel-Strasse Nr. 20 b zu melden.

Ausgenommen sind Geistliche und Kranke mit ärztlichem Attest.

Eventuelles Fernbleiben bezw. Verstoss gegen diesen Befehl, wird strengstens geahndet und zieht Evakuierung und Abkommandierung zum Arbeitseinsatz nach Deutschland nach sich.

Der Kampfkommandant

PRALLE

Kampfkommandantur Venlo

Major

O. U. 20.12.1944.

Threats and reprisals were designed to force the people of Venlo into the labour force.

Short barrels and light-metal gun mounts gave the light artillery a high degree of mobility and a rapid rate of fire.

British Lightnings take over the fighter escort . . .

. . . for the mass drop of Allied airborne units west of Bocholt.

The Assault Battalion (Sturmbatallion) of 1 Parachute Army was attached to the German Pararoop Weapons School in Aalten as a training unit under Hauptmann Eduard Hübner. In February 1945 it was placed under the command of 8 Parachute Division. The Companies of the Assault Battalion were led by Oberleutnants Joswig, Stephan and Pöppel and by Leutnant Sönke.

Two days after Montgomery crossed the Rhine, Rees was still held by the Assault Battalion. Two air-raids and a massive artillery bombardment by the Allies reduced the town to rubble.

Allied amphibious vehicles cross the Rhine at Rees.

For two days there was house to house fighting in Rees.

His Majesty's Own Scottish Regiment takes German paratroopers through Rheinstrasse in Rees, and into captivity.

Prisoner-of-war 'Camp 18', Featherstone Park, Haltwhistle, Northumberland. In these nissen huts were accommodated some three thousand Germans and officers of nations allied to Germany.

Still wearing the black-dyed English 'POW Uniform', Oberleutnant Martin Pöppel (retired) in Ottobrunn near Munich.

Once a parachutist, always a parachutis
Italian jumping competition in Bozen, 19.
On the order of the Allies, Germans were s
not permitted to make jumps over forei
territory, so Martin Pöppel became t
Italian Tino Popelli for the occasio

Post from home was still trickling through. My wife wrote to me: 'Today we are worn out after this terrible hail of bombs. To be hearing the howling of these things all the time, waiting for death at any moment, in a dark cellar, unable to see – oh, it's truly a wonderful life. If only it would stop, they really expect too much of people. Do you still remember the lake? I think you gave me our first kiss there! Everything gone – the lovely cafes Brand and Böhning, the town hall completeley burned. It's impossible even to begin to describe it. But you will be able to imagine it. You have seen Munich. Is everything going to be destroyed? Yet there is no other way out to be seen. Why do people let our soldiers go to their death uselessly, why do they let the rest of Germany be ruined, why all the misery, why?'

On another occasion she wrote: 'Perhaps we won't survive until the end, it is certain that there will be chaos then. And that there will be bloodshed amongst us Germans is obvious, but I won't write any more about that. If you were still a loyal supporter of these people after the war – you know who I mean – it would inevitably separate us. What have they made of our beautiful, magnificent Germany? It's enough to make you weep. And one mustn't even think about how the others will enslave us.'

No, here at the front we mustn't think about it either. Everything had grown so bitter, and we understood the feelings of the people at home, suffered with them and feared for our loved ones who had to bear terror bombing. As far as we were concerned, our only aim now was to bring the men back with as few casualties as possible.

During the slow retreat, there were already obvious signs of disintegration. Bicycles were desperately needed, I knew, since we were still so short of vehicles. But some soldiers were creating mayhem, tearing up the walls and floors of the flimsy houses to look for hidden valuables. It made my blood run cold. In fact I beat hell out of one soldier for doing it, I just couldn't stop myself. Our paratroopers maintained at least some kind of discipline and order, but among other units things were already falling apart.

In February we reached the River Maas in the Reuver-Swalmen region. At this stage we had suffered only light casualties, and the bodies of men killed in action could still be brought back into Germany and buried in Brügge or Bracht. Oberleutnant Becker was killed here, along with the commander of the signal communcation platoon, Oberfeldwebel Stengel. Then back again to the German side of the river, the Lower Rhine side. No more casualties, that was our motto now. All hope of famous victories, the blind obedience, the belief in Germany and the Führer – that had all disappeared.

My batman, a pleasant fair-haired boy, always carried my rucksack with the American sleeping bag I'd captured, cigarettes and cigars, emergency rations and dressings. One day he told me that his home town had already fallen to the enemy and asked if he could push off home to his parents. Although I sympathised with his feelings, I couldn't agree to it. Next night he left with my wonderful rucksack. Sadly, I never heard from him again.

At Alpen we prepared for a counter-attack, to regain Kleve. As we got ready for the attack at Labback/Sonnbeck, the big offensive of Canadian, British and Polish armoured units and infantry began. After days of defensive actions and the forced evacuation of Xanten and Issjum, the battalion withdrew to rear positions in and around Voen. During this fighting, 3 Company under Oberleutnant Stephan was completely destroyed by flame throwing tanks in Martenshof. Shortly afterwards 1 Company under Leutnant Joswig was annihilated between Winstal and Birten, except for one Oberjäger and one Jäger.

I had taken up a position on the periphery, saw the mass tank attack through my field glasses and couldn't do anything about it. An enemy tank on our flank must have seen something glittering in the sun – my field glasses – and sent an armour-piercing shell over which sent the bricks flying around my ears. My helmet got a dent, but I escaped with no more than shock and a long scar. My carelessness with the field glasses had almost cost me my own life and that of many others. Damn it, something like that should never have happened with an old hand like me.

The Reichswald forest was shelled to pieces, shattered, only stumps were left. When the Rhine bridgehead was evacuated, the remainder of the Battalion was among the last German units to cross the river in assault boats at Wesel, on 12 March 1945.

My Company was still almost intact and I was proud of bringing so many men back. Meanwhile, the other Companies had incorporated stragglers to bring their strength up to between 10 and 15 men: consequently, the entire Assault Battalion now had 150 men at its disposal. Astonishingly the enemy failed to pursue us with sufficient force, or else he could have had us all swimming in the Rhine. As a result we got across in good order, had a few days rest and were able to increase the strength of the Battalion with men seconded from various Luftwaffe units. I got two Hauptmann from ground crew. I wondered what to do with them, but eventually decided that they could still be used as messengers. Military police and SS were still strutting around behind the lines, full of self-importance – we reckoned that they'd have done better to be fighting, these blokes.

At Rees-on-Rhine we took up position, with strict orders to hold the town at all costs against the expected major offensive across the Rhine. Our superiors were quick to tell us to hold Rees 'to the last man', but they didn't say what with. About ten kilometres behind us there was a vast quantity of anti-aircraft artillery, but it had the wrong bloody ammunition. What a farce. In Rees there was a bombed-out pipe factory, and we swarmed over the ruins to save a few stems and bowls. We had hardly any rations and so we were forced to pillage the homes of the rich farmers of the Lower Rhine. They still had whole cheeses in their big cellars, at least. Smeared with marmalade, this bread-substitute tasted excellent. The houses were almost all deserted and notes were often stuck to the doors: 'We are out farming by day and come back at night'. That didn't stop the soldiers from taking whatever they could find in the houses, just like they had in Holland. I even caught a teacher thieving and gave him two slaps in the face – unpleasant for him, but definitely better than a court-martial.

In the Pulverturm tower on the bank of the Rhine I set up an observation post, occupied by Willi Rapp and an Obergefreite. We could use the battery commander's telescope to look through the thick cracks and see the British sunning themselves on the other bank of the Rhine. They were as cool as a cucumber. When Rapp opened fire on them with his 5cm mortar, the Tommies hit back with their anti-tank guns and my men soon had to clear out of the tower.

The enemy offensive began on 21 March with a heavy barrage lasting twelve hours. The sky was illuminated by countless rockets and tracer bullets, as if it were a firework display. In the cellar where he had taken cover the candles flickered and were constantly being put out by the blast. Above us the house collapsed so we moved out into the Commander's cellar, though he wasn't there. His wife and Leutnant Giffel were, though. At first we made jokes, but they soon petered out. Suddenly, all our telephone lines were cut. Because of the ceaseless bombardment, the deafening roaring noise, you could hardly make out a single word on the little radio sets. But messengers had to go out, to discover the situation ahead.

We heard that the Tommies had already crossed at Wesel. And five hundred metres to our right they were crossing with amphibious tanks and armoured vehicles. The young Parachute Regiment there hadn't been able to stop them, being unable to realign a lot of our heavy machine-guns, which we had set up for indirect fire on the Rhine. During this period my men could hardly get hold of any rifles or the 8cm mortars with the long barrels, which we had captured from the Russians. The Commander managed to break through to us during a lull in the shooting, but in all honesty there was nothing left here to lead. All we could do was wait for the infantry attack. Now they were advancing on the city from all sides. Then, in glorious weather, a whole armada of paratroopers dropped about ten kilometres behind us.

We were completely surrounded.

After the war, the engineer Professor Ernst Ulreich Reuther wrote to me that the horror would have been even greater for the small Assault Battalion, except for its courage and readiness to let itself be destroyed for its comrades. He was right. We were determined to hang on, not to surrender. The house-to-house fighting raged through Rees for days, from street to street. Hand grenades could be a lethal weapon in these conditions, when thrown over a wall into a group of enemy soldiers. These goddamned Tommies – we were determined they wouldn't get us.

Since there was little he could do here, the Commander decided to break out and try to re-establish control from a new position. I decided to stay put. The battle for Rees lasted almost three days, during which time we hung on grimly and gave our other troops the chance to continue the battle behind us.

The 'Illustrated London News', 7 April 1945: '. . . the 1st Battalion the Gordon Highlanders cleared the last Germans out of the north-eastern quarter of Rees on March 26. It has been an all in fight, from street to street and house to house, for 51 hours, against 500 to 600 fanatic young enemy paratroopers.' The reporter exaggerated our numbers, perhaps in an attempt to explain why an entire British Division had failed to break through. There were maybe 180 of us in all. We sent out recce patrols under experienced Feldwebel and Oberjäger to discover if there was any chance of a break-out, but it was hopeless. Most of them suffered heavy casualties, or failed to return altogether.

I discussed the situation with the last Unteroffizier. The Führer order was very much in my mind: 'If a superior officer no longer appears in a position to lead, he is to hand over command to the nearest rank below.' Personally, I was ready to surrender – me, who had been a paratrooper from the very first day of the war. Yet although the struggle was completely hopeless, men came to me in tears. 'As paratroopers, how will we be able to look our wives in the face, if we surrender voluntarily.' A phenomenon, incredible. I had lived through the incredible inhumanity of war, experienced its highs and – for months – its lows, the horrors and the hell. And at the end of it all, to be confronted by this attitude. Then, after long silence, they said that if the 'Old Man' (it would have been funny if it wasn't so sad, that I was the Old Man at the age of 24) – if I thought we should surrender, then they would follow me.

It happened quickly. I gave the order to hide all valuables and to put on double clothing. My batman asked me if he could break open an officer's chest. Yes. I took an anti-aircraft officer's good cloth coat – may he forgive me – and a briefcase in which I put my few belongings. Waving a white cloth on a broom handle, we emerged towards the Tommies, who were advancing on our last position. A hefty Sergeant and a whole load of Tommies kept their submachine guns trained on us, and only stopped being afraid of a few paratroopers when they saw that we weren't carrying any weapons. We were surrounded, frisked and if anybody was careless enough to be still wearing a watch, it was quickly taken. Bloody fool, I was! I had reminded my men to hide their valuables but had failed to take my own advice.

The fighting was over for us at last. First of all we were taken through the shattered streets of Rees to the Oldenkott tobacco factory. There were very few survivors from the light infantry companies and the staff company, and my 4 Company again had fewest casualties. All the officers except me (was I too cowardly, too careful, too clever?) were dead. I had time to exchange a few words, then we were taken across the Rhine to fields which had been fenced off. On one side the Unteroffizier and other ranks, and me on the other side, completely alone like a cow in the pasture. A lot of men quickly shoved their paybooks under the fence so that I could promote them. I promoted all of them, no ordinary soldier has ever been made an Oberjäger so quickly. Whether it was for prestige, or for increased POW pay, I didn't mind. I was taken to an omnibus, completely filled with files. A British Captain, speaking good German, told me: 'Now we've got you, we only need Hauptmann Hüber.' Then he took a file, skimmed through, and read out details of the positions of the Battalion, my own career and our casualties – fairly accurate right up to the last day.

Well, that's certainly one way to wage war. When they took us away, we drove past kilometre after kilometre of Allied artillery positions, thousands of guns. With us it was always 'Sweat Saves Blood', but with them it was 'Equipment Saves Men'. Not with us. We didn't need equipment, did we? After all, we were heroes.

They transported us through Holland and Belgium on open goods wagons. The people there, bitter at their fate, threw stones at us from roads or bridges, but not many reached their target. Vae victis. The long years of war had so demoralised us that we had nothing left. They could do with us whatever they wanted with us. Along with a few others I was picked out and brought to an airfield. We were taken to London in an aircraft filled with wounded Tommies, to begin our period of captivity.

In Captivity – March 1945

I think it was called Wolverhampton Park, the place where I spent ten wonderful days. My own room, white linen on the bed, my own batman, ham and eggs for breakfast. Then interrogation. For two hours every day a British Captain – he had studied in Heidelberg before the war – talked with me. Not about the war as such, not about the operations, weapons and equipment. Instead, he wanted to see into the heart and soul of a young (and in his opinion still fanatical) officer of Hitler. He was friendly and matter-of-fact, gentlemanlike is the term we use in Germany too, offering Chesterfield and Woodbine cigarettes. I didn't care what he thought, and I said things as I saw them. He tried patiently to show me the evil of the Hitler regime, but failed because of my obstinacy and a kind of blind Nibelungen loyalty which still held me in its grip. I had survived, but I didn't see any reason for me to crawl to these moneybags, however friendly they were. I wasn't going to say to them 'You are right, of course you are right'.

Only – they were right, although I did not know it then, or didn't want to admit it. In those early days I still couldn't see how the German people had been misused. But my fiancée had no need to be afraid any more. In February she had written to me, you see, to tell me that 'If you were to remain a loyal supporter of these people after the war – you know who I mean – then it would inevitably part us'.

In all honesty, women have more understanding. We men had been educated to stubborn, blind obedience. By the end of the war I had certainly become more critical, but cured – completely cured – I was not. However, it was not to take much longer before I recognised the truth. The game of interrogation ended and I spent a short time in a small camp. Small, but ah, with the best of company. One-man U Boat operators, frogmen, Waffen-SS, some paratroopers, apparently all 'Black' (translator's note: that is, regarded by the Allies as fanatical Nazis). Yet somehow the interrogating officer – I recognised him on the television in 1981 – had discovered some spark in me and had noted it because, along with some others, I was transferred to the 'Whites' and moved to another camp.

The train travelled by night. A pity, because we couldn't see anything. We got out in Newcastle, not far from the border between England and Scotland. On the Tyne there was Featherstone Park, a big officers' camp for 3500 people, near a boarding school in a castle which had once been acquired by Lord Nelson for Lady Hamilton. A forest of Nissen huts, each containing fifty men. We had a rough time for a number of weeks, but let's face it – we could hardly expect hotel accommodation.

There were some fine men, good comrades among the prisoners there, but there was also a whole crowd of dirty little rats, especially among the middle-ranking staff officers. If my faith in German people had already been crumbling before, now whole walls of conviction started to collapse. We saw fat Obersts bending down to pick up the glowing dog-ends dropped by British Sergeants, even running and scrambling after them, we saw men denouncing others and being denounced by them, and all this was happening among men who were supposed to be officer-comrades. For many of us, it was the end of all our illusions. A fine mountain infantry Hauptman, whose shoe-shop in Munich's Augustenstrasse I was later to patronise frequently, was denounced by fellow German officers for some thoughtless remark he had made. A few days later I saw him again, covered with bandages and plasters, all his front teeth knocked out. The notorious Sergeant-thugs had really beaten him up badly. Or take our 'East Markers', the Austrians ('East Mark' was the Nazi name for Austria after Hitler had annexed it as part of the German Reich – translator's note). Well, we could understand it when one of them came to us and said 'Listen, if say I'm loyal to Austria, then maybe they'll let me go home earlier'. That was in order. But 80% of them were now contemptuous of us 'Germans', as though their men and ours had never fought and died together such a short time before, or as though we had never exchanged friendly 'Heil Hitler' greetings. The Hungarian officers were different. They stood loyally by us, though God knows they were no Nazis. No, in that camp I saw whole worlds collapse. There were not many paratroopers there: their army was already in Valhalla.

After a while a new Camp Commandant arrived, an older Colonel who had been a prisoner of the Germans in both the First and Second World Wars and had been well treated by them. In return, he was determined to be fair to us. Our rations and camp life also improved. After the film about the Bergen-Belsen concentration camp, we were forced to watch in a nearby cinema, we also had more understanding for the beatings we received from Jewish guards. Knowing what they knew, what co-operation could we expect to get from them? But the new Commandant had been a soldier all his life and he regarded us as soldiers too, not as Nazis. German assistants were soon assigned to the English camp police, and I was among the men who used this opportunity to improve my English. Soon the prisoners were allowed to take complete responsiblity for camp patrols. At the end of 1945 we were also allowed – under supervision – to go in groups into the nearby village. Jesus, the people here were poor. Oil lamps, open fires, wretched houses. No wonder that the Tommies were keen to get hold of everything that we had. Even simple pens found a ready market. In the great colonial Empire, it seemed that only the High Society was wealthy.

Through the good offices of the Commandant, we gradually smartened up our camp. He got hold of dyestuffs, bags, chests, materials and tools for use and we used them for handicrafts, transforming the huts into attractive, light and homely dwellings. We made armchairs, cupboards, panelled furniture and much more. One day I tried to make a chair, but one leg was always too short, so I sawed so much off that eventually I ended up with a footstool. We organised competitions to spur ourselves on to more civilised living, and after my captivity I would have been happy to have lived in such an attractive litle room. Even the noise of the card-players around me didn't matter. Notoriously stubborn as ever, I was still determined to bone up on my English.

The generous supply of materials allowed us to create stages, reading rooms, rooms for religious worship. The last were especially well used, particularly as there were army chaplains among the prisoners. Many adherents of the Nazi church found their way back to their true God during this period, and why not? Personally, I had left the Church during the war and had never prayed for my life even during the worst moments. Even today, I still have no need for any Church.

On the four stages we built, a programme worthy of a thriving city was being offered. The Gipsy Baron, Die Fledermaus, Frau Luna etc – we managed to stage them all. The few women's roles were acted very artistically, without seeming ludicrous or mawkish. In the next theatre there were classics such as Richard III and Don Juan, in the next we laughed at popular shows like 'The Gasman' or 'Johann Has An Idea'. Lively orchestras too – one man in a room nearby was a real gipsy and played the fiddle. There was chamber music on

Sunday mornings, music for strings, and dance music in the afternoons to make us forget everything and transport us into the dream world of home. But the most important creation was our Ministry of Education and the Arts, which offered high-quality teachers and professors and an excellent programme of study. Courses for holders of the school leaving examination, for the occupation of landlord – including practical work in the kitchen, for structural and civil engineering, for the breeding of domestic animals (at home we would learn to value this knowledge), for architects, student teachers, bookkeepers, doctors – everything was on offer. Courses of lectures in at least ten languages – I took Portuguese, of all things – lectures in history, history of art, social sciences and economics. All these courses, and we were avid to learn, to satisfy our starved brains.

But it was not only our spiritual and intellectual needs that were catered for. We could also volunteer for labour duties which, according to the Geneva Convention, were not compulsory for officers. But we were desperate to get physical work, since then you could get out of the camp and get in touch with the local farmers who could provide us with many extras. The men from our room reported for road-building work on an airfield. That was, or at any rate soon turned into, quite an experience. We were allowed to work at our own discretion, without any supervision, 'You Germans can do everything anyway, you'll do it right'. It was foggy in the field and I thought I'd take the chance to have a look around. There was a barracks there. From the window, pretty British girls in uniforms offered me cigarettes and we talked. A comrade had given me a cigarette case he had made, so I was keen to give this in return. One of the girls was so thrilled by the pretty box that she gave me half a packet of cigarettes. That's really something, I thought, kept it to myself for the rest of the day, and only told my comrades about it when we were back at camp that evening. Of course, the incident had given me an idea . . . We collected half a sackful of our handicrafts, went to the barracks again the next day, and came back with packets of cigarettes, coffee, tea and chocolate. The girls were especially keen to have little puppets, so we tailored supply to meet demand and I organised the manufacture of these figures on a kind of assembly line in the barracks, the heads from papier maché and the clothes from remnants of material. But selling from hand to hand like that wasn't good enough for me – I wanted to do it on a much grander scale. Once I'd managed to convince a Sergeant of the guard (with a little assistance) of the benefits of this business, I had it made. As a result, I opened my shop on two long tables in the guard room – just imagine it – and it flourished!

This happy state of affairs lasted for a week, but then our good Commandant decided to pay a call on his road-builders and – unfortunately – he walked straight into my shop. This was definitely going too far. The shop was closed and I, escorted by soldiers, received four weeks confinement to barracks and a reduced cigarette ration. The last of these punishments wasn't too hard to bear though, since I already had stocks laid in.

For weeks there had been an obstinate latrine rumour that we were soon to be released. However well things were going, the idea was always in the forefront of our minds. Our rations were now excellent, plentiful and good. The porridge, often with raisins, tasted wonderful and on Sundays we got four or five slices of cake. Every month, we could order any clothing that was missing and it was usually delivered promptly. Almost all of us possessed his own dyed English suit and shoes, and we could get our washing done in English laundries for a small fee. When we thought of home, we couldn't imagine that things could be better there. But we wanted to go home, we wanted to build, to work.

English newspapers were available, and we translated them avidly for the latest news from home. The post – that magic word – produced hope and dread, joy and grief. For many of our comrades from the Russian-occupied areas, for our East Prussians, Pomeranians, Silesians, and Sudeten Germans, there was hardly any news at all. They still didn't know whether their families had got out, or even if there were alive. Their heads dropped when one of us got post, and they had to hide their tears and their fear. I had managed to write my first card months before, when the Morgenthau Plan was on everyone's lips. It said simply: 'Healthy – everything all right – hope the same with you'.

On 12 November 1945 I received some post from home to say that everyone was well and finally, on 17th January 1946, a card arrived from my fiancée to say that she was all right too. A great weight was lifted from my mind with the news that everyone was still alive. I wrote immediately to say that Gerda should go with her brother from Magdeburg to Ottobrunn as they'd be safer there. She was anxious about my parents, who were Nazis in a very minor way, and she told me how she hoped that the current pathetic outbreak of slander and abuse among the Germans would end soon. The food supply was poor and they were just hoping to survive the summer and autumn. The news from home, gleaned partly from letters and mainly from English newspapers, was so disturbing that we POWs found ourselves writing to tell them: 'Chins up, we're coming soon'.

An astonishing transformation had taken place, encouraged by the fair treatment we were getting. At the end of the war we were completely demoralised, but after some time in captivity we began to grow stronger all the time. Somehow, the spirit of battle had been reawakened by the sufferings of home. Perhaps we were just stubborn, not prepared to accept the collapse of our world, the devaluation of all values. In any case, we were drawing new strength from these setbacks. The vast majority of us were soldiers, often credulous soldiers, but not executioners and not monsters. We had been committed to Germany, but now we had to find new meaning in our lives. Each one of us would have to struggle alone for himself and his family without being able to stand shoulder-to-shoulder with other soldiers, without the comradeship of proud elite troops to support us.

But there seemed to be no prospect of repatriation. England needed its galley slaves and broken Germany was giving the remainder of its sons to provide them. One of them hanged himself, a teacher, Nazi official, father of three: in flight from his feelings of guilt, cowardice about his life and despair that he couldn't fulfil his responsibilities towards his family. Today a subject of table talk, tomorrow forgotten.

One day I joined the Democratic Working Group' (the object of much derision among the POWs), as an end in itself and out of interest in its goals, especially in economic reconstruction. Since everything had been destroyed, bombed, demolished, then perhaps – but only perhaps – we might get the chance to become competitive with the most modern machinery. We'd see.

My third interrogation did not go well. Paratroopers, especially those he thought were committed to the Nazi Church, were too much for the good civilian, who was still convinced that the wolves needed to be reformed. There is an expression which is highly appropriate here: 'Go and kiss my arse'. On another occasion I paid one more visit to the camp doctor, Dr Neumann, because of the injury to my head. This brought on another dose of repatriation-itis, of course. The following week I was to be examined by an English doctor at a clinic in Newcastle. Keep your fingers crossed for me!

Material from an essay or an idea I had: 'The POWs among themselves'. If anyone thinks that the life of the POW is steady and calm, I'm afraid that they're very much mistaken. Perhaps some of you believe that life behind the barbed wire brings out the best attributes of the stronger sex, and that true manliness is revealed because the POWs are not subjected to the pernicious influences of women. If so, I'm afraid I must disappoint you. God gave man a wife for good reason. Men amongst themselves, and under such hard conditions, seem to need to outdo each other, to act as a mirror image of the divine Zeus. But what are they really like? Poor figures, wretched products of nature, playthings of the ego. 'Only in the field is man worth something.' The composer was not a POW, otherwise he would have celebrated the men behind the barbed wire.

Now to comment on the individual POW. He showed himself best, and most clearly, as a being capable of adjusting to any situation. You could say that he had developed into a chameleon. Youths became men, grown men grew childish again like schoolboys, the warrior turned meek as a lamb, the Nazi Party bigwig was transformed into an eternal democrat etc, etc. The ability to adjust was the secret, was the key to the repatriation camp. There were lone wolves and crowds, small groups and larger bands of like-minded men, stupid men and intellectuals (as well as those who thought they were), notorious layabouts and hard-workers. Many people moved between these categories. They belonged to one group for some time, switched to the next and then returned to their old group. Slowly but surely, each one shed his skin. There was plenty of time for such thoughts behind the wire.

Yes, I could understand them, although today comprehension comes only with difficulty. And I saw a special danger that even the good men among the Blacks might become embittered as the years pass, increasingly sterile and irresponsible. When we looked around, what room was there for such defiance, just a pinprick against a wall of steel? They may have dreamt of a secret German resistance movement, but that wasn't real soldiering, it was just playing at soldiers. The armies of occupation wouldn't tolerate anarchy, and God knows they had the means to impose their will. Comrades, this wasn't the way. We needed men to roll up their shirt sleeves and get to work on reconstruction. Germany had had enough of cops-and-robbers games. Personal responsibility, which the 'Führer' took away from us, could no longer be avoided.

There were other differences between Whites and Blacks. Often the Whites were bureaucrats, these 'completely innocent' men who never killed anyone or even caused anyone injury. They had only removed a couple of trains full of 'booty' from the occupied countries or brought a couple of trucks out, full of 'Old Napoleon'. There were even general staff officers among them, who somehow managed to claim that they had nothing to do with militarism. A crazy world.

There was one further group. I've already written about the Austrians and the Hungarians, but there were also the Bavarians, not many, but some, who demanded the re-establishment of the old Bavarian republic. For them, Hitlerism was a Prussian invention. Maybe so, but wasn't Munich the birthplace of the Nazi Party? The most harmless among the 'foreigners' were the supporters of the Rhenish-Catholic Union. They fluctuated between wanting their own Constitution, rule by the Frenchies and papal dominion – they were idiots.

Now for the Greys. About this group there was no real agreement. Their previous political history might perhaps have been assessed as 'good', but it wasn't outstanding. Nevertheless they were hopeful, always excessively polite, protested their innocence and claimed that their membership of the Nazi Party was forced on them in order to secure their livelihood. However, this group also included many men who could honestly listen to reason, realise the truth and admit it. You could call them 'political pupils on an advanced course of retraining'.

And now for the Blacks. They created a class among and for themselves and were the masters, the proud ones, the idealists. Not one bowed head, not one democratic whimper, only discipline and order. They allowed themselves few hopes of an early return home and lived for each other, calm, heroic. They did not realise, and had no desire to understand, that they were lying to themselves. For them all explanations were a swindle, the war and its end were the unjust judgement of the world, and the Nazi system remained their ideal. On the 'Führer's Birthday' they appeared in their smartest uniform, with white gloves if possible, stood to attention and thought in silence of their leader.

Once he had been mine too, but was so no longer. What was especially tragic was that these idealists were often potentially among the best men. They withdrew from life and thought that this made them better Germans than the rest. They didn't see that the best men were most desperately needed at home, not the bootlickers and the disloyal ones. But with their attitude, with their Nibelungen-style loyalty, they hadn't got a chance.

People with no faith in Germany's future had to make plans for their parents, brothers and sister, wives and children, for their friends and their wounded comrades. They had to plan for the future but not try to evoke and re-create a defeated past. Many of these 'Blacks' seemed to me like children who want their broken toy mended, not like men who could draw new strength from mistakes and setbacks. But I could understand them. After all, in 1943 I displayed the same stubbornness towards the man who was later to be my father-in-law, during a visit to Magdeburg. There was a big globe standing on a desk which he pointed to with his finger, showing how small Germany was, and then made a large circle: 'And do "they" want to conquer it all?' This comment didn't go down well with me – I was a proud Leutnant in the paratroops in those days.

Without my mordant sense of humour, I think I would have despaired. It wasn't life as a POW that had this effect, but the intentions and well-meaning plans of the occupying powers. In my view, the Russians were behaving like Asiatic hordes, as the English newspapers confirmed; we were offended when the French sent negroes from Senegal to occupy our homeland; we thought America was sadistically bent on destroying us; only England seemed to be pursuing a benevolent policy, but only a policy. They should have followed it earlier under their 'great Churchill', and not let the Russians advance to the Elbe by demanding unconditional surrender. Did they think that Stalin – a worthy and more cunning successor to Ivan the Terrible – would ever leave the areas he conquered? It wasn't just Communism, but also the ancient Russian drive for expansion. I wasn't gloating, because I'd made more than my share of mistakes, but the Churchills and Roosevelts did not behave in a European way. To give up half of Europe because of Hitler and to hand it over to Stalin, that really wasn't 'grand policy'.

Germany suffering from inflation, hunger, cold, plunder – powerless and without honour. Vansittart was raging, de Gaulle made bitter-sweet speeches, and Morgenthau wanted to turn us into day labourers and peasants. The Anglo-Saxon world raged at Moscow – too late; Moscow yapped back – they had what they wanted. The Russians had reached the Turkish border, 'liberated' politicians were fleeing, from Poland, Rumania etc. A witches' sabbath for the whole world. I'm sure I could hear Satan laughing. Emotions fluctuated as the weeks passed. Pacifist and blood lust, hedonist and recluse, communist or anarchist, sometimes even democrat. Everything unripe, there'd be no harvest until we got home.

Our model democrat Hans Thaler, manager of the sales articles for soldiers, embezzled a packet of tobacco. Not that this was anything out of the ordinary among our little officer elite, nor that I was shocked about it on that account. But we all knew about his character, the way he denied his Germanness, and his democratic whimperings. The most astonishing thing about the whole affair was the opinion of our camp leader, Oberst Primus. In his view, the embezzlement 'of such a feeble little packet' was really not so terrible, and he dismissed Thaler with honour and regret because of the 'lack of proof'. Was *that* an officer's spirit from a serving officer? Oh my Germany, what has become of you?

My birthday was celebrated rather more noisily than I originally wanted. I was woken up by music from my comrades and my room-mates gave me coffee and cigarettes, actually an indirect invitation to a coffee party. Teddy Schott turned up with a lively three-man band and everyone had a wonderful time. Summa summarum, I was left with five cigarettes, and the swine had swindled us out of our tobacco ration for three weeks.

Christmas. A short, effective and profound speech from the prince of our hut, Hauptmann Brechlin, followed by Christmas carols, poems and stories to put us in the right mood. Amazing and fortunate how these little festivals could help turn our communities' pain into joy. Mauer was very successful as Father Christmas, presents with both material and sentimental value exchanged, there was a great deal of singing and laughter. But the best time was when Schröder played his harmonica as we lay in our beds, hands crossed behind our heads, dreaming of home. That Christmas we produced a Christmas newspaper including a comic poem about me, describing me as a Communist-hating pacifist who tried to evade all orders of whatever sort, but particularly when they involved my turn at firelighting duty.

Soon after that the first 100 of our wounded and sick were on their way home, getting the repatriation they deserved, poor blokes. I was due to go to the doctor again, determined to keep on trying. But then we heard that in summer a large number of us would be released. The craziest, most exciting and detailed rumours circulated and multiplied. Of course they were passed on in secret, because their author was determined to extract the last cigarettes in return for his information. But – and this was new – we heard there was an actual list with release dates for Groups A-K, who were to be repatriated by June. This included, first and foremost, more wounded men and the permanently sick or disabled, along with older men and boys. And then – a bitter-sweet secret – nobody knew what would happen after that.

Politically reliable men, or men with specific professional skills? Men selected by Zones, or by age? Our spies couldn't find out for certain how the repatriation lists were designed, what the Groups meant. Anyway, it seemed certain that none of the Groups would apply to me, except perhaps the one for the wounded. I was a paratrooper, 25 years old, a German Christian, former leader of a Hitler Youth unit although in only a minor way. Surely that would put me in group 'Z', however the lists were compiled. That night I dreamed of travelling to the coast in a heated carriage, full of hope. Damn this shit, damn these rumours.

Next we heard that 3000 brown battledresses had been ordered, without patches. This could surely only be to go home in. And last of all, the Commandant was supposed to have said that the interrogations should be over in seven weeks (which must mean by mid-March). So if I was really lucky after all, I could be skiing in the fields near home that month.

There was a sensational article in one of the newspapers shortly before that. The Zurich newspaper 'Weltwoche' of 16 November 1945 was describing life in the territories now occupied by Poland. The Swiss correspondent specifically stated that he was telling the absolute truth. He wrote of the land of death between the Vistula and the Oder – a land without law and justice, without human dignity. The Germans outlawed, hunted, killed, plundered, raped, starved. Many typhus villages hermetically sealed off from the outside world, no assistance for them. Corpses in rows in the streets, children less than a year old starved to death, little girls and women raped. Fair game for organised gangs. People who didn't leave voluntarily were starved out, and those who remained were outlawed. No judges, no authorities, no police helped them. Mass flight and mass death, this was the fate of the German population in purely German areas, not even in Polish ones.

No comment necessary.

Gerdl, my little blonde girl, why didn't you walk in stocking-feet to Munich? To think of you among the Russians was unbearable. (Later I was to find out how women and girls disguised themselves, smeared themselves with filth, to avoid attracting attention.) One man from our hut, Leutnant Schunk, was a Sudeten German. Where could he go? I told him that after he was released he must come to me in Bavaria. The ones like me, who were lucky enough to live in the US Zone, we simply had to help wherever we can. In all this hatred of everything and everybody, you simply didn't let a good comrade down.

The 8 March, a memorable day in my life as a POW. In the evening I was told that I would be sent home in the next few days. An incredible thought, I just couldn't grasp that I was going home – home at last. I couldn't believe it, and pinched my cheeks to make sure that I wasn't dreaming. But it was a fact, the order was there. I could write page after page about this moment, about the hopes and feelings connected with it. Home – a magic word. I was cruelly woken from my daydreams when our 'War Criminals Club' teased me – telling me that I mustn't believe it, not for a moment, since it couldn't be true. These rats, to make me full of doubts.

Everything OK at the clothing parade. I met Major Neumann, the 'Red Chief' of B-Camp, who was also going home. Next morning we were among the 60 men standing in front of the Camp Commandant, Lieutenant Colonel Vickers, with Captain Sulzbach translating. (Translator's note: Herbert Sulzbach was born a German Jew and served in the German Army in the trenches during the First World War. Forced to flee Germany to escape Nazi persecution, he served with the British Army during the Second World War and, after its end, worked in POW camps for reconciliation and understanding between peoples. He has been awarded decorations by several countries, including Germany and France, for his efforts.) Lieutenant Colonel Vickers told us that under his leadership and with our good conduct, the Camp had improved its position. Six months ago the camp had still been surrounded with three tanks of high barbed wire with watch-towers; today there was only a wire fence, and we were permitted unsupervised walks up to eight kilometres away. Sport, conversation, and work had made our lives as prisoners more tolerable. After two wars, he saw it as his life's task to treat German officers decently and to send them home as quickly as possible. When educating our children, he hoped that we would remember the immense suffering of these two wars, and teach them to be friends of peace and friends of England. 'We must come together.' These words, spoken by an honourable soldier, made a deep impression on us. Even the most inveterate enemies of England would not forget him, nor what he said.

I didn't say much to my comrades, I can understand how they felt. An old Hauptmann said that it would be unjust to send the boys home and not him, an old man. I couldn't help remarking that he should have gone to the front to make sure he got a 'repatriation wound' which would have solved his problem. I exchanged addresses with my comrades and I packed my gear, giving my stuff away wherever possible. Then my friends gave me a last poem, with an attractive border and comical illustrations, about my Bavarian blood, my eagerness to go on courses in the camp, and telling me to remember them when I got home:

> . . . Lasst uns schïteln deine Händ
> und zu Haus im Glück
> denk an uns zurück
>
> Let us shake you by the hands
> And when you are at home in joy
> Think back and remember us . . .

All these fine fellows, as young as I was – I had to leave them behind, hoping against hope that they would soon be following me. 3500 officers should have been a real elite. Many were not worthy of that, but the others, the few, made up for them.

By train to a camp in the south of England, next day on a Liberty Ship. In its enormous belly we all looked for somewhere to sit, daydreamed, still almost unable to believe that we were crossing to Germany!

The Elbe, Hamburg. Disembarkation.

On 20th March I was already in Munster transit camp. The mood here was almost unbelievable, completely apathetic and hidebound. There were a lot of older men, many old officers, shabby to look at. I was almost ashamed that I once wore that uniform. Perhaps the mood was a consequence of the impression that we received even at the station. Everywhere there were just women and boys working in patched old uniforms, examining bricks, searching through the ruins for anything that could be used. Then the train journey with its unending procession of shattered towns, villages, factories – for all our joy at coming home, the sight made us draw in our breaths. We passed numerous goods trains full of machines, all destined for abroad – it made us fear for the future. But who knows, maybe this removal of the machinery from all our factories would be for the best, maybe one day we'd be able to beat the others hollow with our own brand-new machinery. At the time, this defiance felt like whistling in the dark. The city was dead, but life round the barracks continued with its own weird vitality. Tommies walked around in all their finery, with collars and ties, a German 'Fräulein' on their arm. Elsewhere groups of people were just standing around and talking, some speaking of another war. The prevailing tone was of misery. What was there to lose that they hadn't lost already? And there were black marketeers, cigarettes dangling from the corner of their big mouths, waiting for customers with eyes drooping and almost closed. Cigarettes here cost 7 Marks a packet, a day's pay. Who on earth could afford that?

Farmers and peasants, mainly from the lost territories in the east, were easy to recognise with their sturdy frames and clumsy movements. What did folk do the whole day long? Why, they just watched other people. Our own administration here in the camp was useless and indifferent to our fate. Most were young lads, real braggarts who would rather sell our rations than look after us. After all, they told us, we, not they, were the people who prolonged the war. Little wonder that we were more hungry than we had been for a long time. To feed 100 men there was biscuits in tins, handed out after half a litre of dreadful ersatz coffee (reminding me how delicious the tea was in Merry Old England) had been poured into each man's tin, jam jar or even mess-tin. At midday half a litre of milk, watered down of course, a wafer-thin bread soup, in the evening three slices of bread, 20g butter, 50g vegetables and that delicious broth again. After a few days many of us, including me, found that when we got up in the morning everything went black in front of our eyes. Lethargy tended to spread, many men stayed in bed or dozed the whole day long. In the daytime it was better anyway, you could at least sleep. In these two barrack blocks there were at least 2600 men, with 200 men crammed into each room. No light, no oil heater, no beds, not even plank beds. Each man lay wrapped in his blanket on the hard floor. Some snored like horses, others wheezed like men with diseased lungs, somebody else let off a fart like thunder. Now if you were very unlucky and got a bloke with a diseased bladder behind you, then things were really bad. He'd have to climb over everyone in the middle of the night, was sure to hit somebody in the ribs, step on someone else's finger or toe. Then there'd be a real row. 'Lift your legs up, you stupid oaf', 'haven't you got eyes in your head, you arsehole', and colourful dialect oaths from some of my fellow Bavarians and Swabians here. When the culprit finally got outside, everyone simmered down and we'd all turn over and try to snatch a little more sleep – until the next man had to go out, since this went on for half the night.

When we woke up, we were all still exhausted. Only the bravest men among us could face going out to wash. There was a stable with long wooden benches, where between 800 and 1000 men had to fight in the dark for the four taps. Consquently, many men didn't get up until later or didn't bother to wash at all, making do with rubbing a facecloth over their eyes. And then the stink when they emerged from their blankets – God, it certainly wasn't a perfume counter.

I felt particularly sorry for the sick, the mutilated, and the cripples because they had it hardest of all. In this place, where nobody knew anyone else, nobody helped anyone else either. Each man was his own nearest and dearest. What had happened to the ideal of comradeship? Over in England things had gone well for us, and even the few men from Russian camps said that they were treated at least half-way decently. Many of the men with gastric disorders, rheumatism, amputations had already been waiting for weeks in the most appalling conditions. It was just a transit camp, and no one felt any responsibility for conditions there. I was surprised that the British didn't intervene, since they were so fair to us over there. In the queue for rations things were really insane. You had to watch for the queue-jumpers, the crafty types, who would push stealthily forward if people didn't stop them. A lot of people always went short because they failed to curse and swear whenever the man distributing the food made a tiny mistake. The queue-jumpers had it off pat – 'he's got one spoon too many', or 'my soup is too thin', 'why don't you begin with me?' or 'I've only got a small mug' (he had another one in his other hand, behind his back). Not surprising that one of the helpers flew off the handle once and threw a full tureen of food into the face of one of the noisiest moaners. But all that good soup going to waste! I decided to make a move. It worked, and I got some of it for myself, even though it was only lukewarm. The cold food was distributed in a calmer atmosphere because nobody got second helpings of that, except for the biscuits, when everyone was careful to ensure that nobody got a crumb too much. Are animals as brutal as this?

If the weather was barely tolerable, we got out in the yard to walk off our 1000 calories, otherwise we'd have got too fat, of course. Then one of the proud possessors of cigarettes would get one out and blow the smoke gleefully under the noses of all of us with none. There was almost murder done then – these plutocrats. If you tried to ask for one or do a swap for one – no, it was always the last he had. But occasionally a comradely type might get hold of half a fag, and then he'd strike a match and pass it round to share.

You could recognise the good old soldiers, because they steadfastly continued to clean, polish and wash their gear. Many of them still had a chessboard, like me, or a pack of cards. When the men weren't sleeping or dozing, they gathered into groups to discuss things. But we didn't have intelligent conversations. It was better to talk about gardening, breeding of small animals (rabbits), since we would soon need these skills, or about distilling and the cultivation of tobacco. There were eminent authorities on these subjects among us. A lot of people just stood at the window, dreaming of the freedom we all longed for.

At the beginning of April it arrived, in the shape of a goods train to transport us to the American Zone, prepared for about 1200 men. The accompanying staff were drawn from among our own ranks. We were just short of a bugler, so I immediately stuck up my hand to volunteer. If they only knew that I'd never so much as raised a cornet to my lips! Anway, I went with the others to a catering coach, to help with the distribution of rations. It was fair – there was plenty left over for everyone. And as we were all starving, we spread the butter deep and thick on the biscuits and stuffed ourselves. Like the others, I quickly regretted it.

On 5 April we reached Cassel. The weather was beautiful, though a little cold. Treysa, Marburg lying prettily among the hills. Bad Beuheim was less shattered than other places. People waved at us as we passed. In Hanau the fruit trees were already in blossom – incredible what a difference these glorious red and white flowers made. Our mood of spring and homecoming grew, and was further encouraged when the people in Giessen stood waving to us, making us feel genuinely welcome home. At the station they gave us newspapers and piles of cigarettes, and we repaid the children by giving them crispbread.

At one level-crossing, dozens of girl factory workers were waiting to see us, to the delight of the thirsty soldiery. That afternoon we passed Aschaffenburg and then our last camp of Babenhausen, still in Hessen. It was a tented camp under Polish supervision, but with SS staff. Here things were dominated by order and discipline, where before there had been none. And American standards of hygiene, with disinfectants in the latrines, de-lousing stations, DDT cabins, adequate washing facilities. And then the rations. In the morning we got semolina, at lunchtime there was thick pea soup, in the evening white bread, sausage and cheese and – genuine pure coffee. That's right, real coffee. Unfortunately I didn't get to eat many of these delicacies. I was stuffed so full of that damned butter that I was forced to set up my personal encampment right by the latrines, which I visited almost continuously. Those three days were absolutely, literally, the shits. I was completely worn out, finished.

On the last day I finally began to enjoy that wonderful 'Ami' food, then we were told to report for our discharge papers. Although we were prepared, it was still quite an experience! A couple of hundred men in three rows, carrying rucksacks, seabags, cardboard boxes or just holdalls. I had been able to save my seabag, still fairly tighly packed.

First rank five paces forwards, baggage on the ground! What was I seeing? Supervised by beefy US Sergeants, the bags were being emptied and everything that seemed necessary for our freedom was taken away. A groundswell of muttering, which died away again in the fear that we might not be released after all. What brave little lambs we had become, we wolves. But I was still able to judge the situation coolly, a talent that I'd either been born with or had learned in the war. When the friskers came to the end of the first rank, I simply took my baggage calmly in my hand and walked cheerfully forward into it. By the right, quick march, and we were outside. I was free and still had my nice full seabag. I've often laughed about this delightful trick. They should have known, you can't treat an old paratrooper like that!

The rest is soon told.

A last handshake, 'good luck, keep in touch', and a couple of us boarded an Ami-truck which took us to the station. A tall negro with a big friendly smile was our driver. Train to Munich, then on foot to the other station, the Ostbahnhof. My home city, once so beautiful, lay in ruins. Though I had become hardened to such sights, I wasn't ashamed to cry. Starving, careworn faces, clothes patched a thousand times, amputees on primitive crutches, old women carrying things home through the ruins on prams or little handcarts. But also, in many people, the desire to rebuild. Large numbers knocking down the walls of ruined buildings, fetching pipes and everything else that might be of use, knocking the old plaster off bricks.

Nobody recognised me in the little slow train to the suburb of Ottobrunn. Tanned, with a jaunty moustache, in my black POW uniform with my shabby old cap pulled down – who on earth could recognise me? When the train approached the station, I grew so scared that the sweat broke out on my forehead. Where they all still alive, was my parents' little shop still standing?

It was still there. I had come home.

Oberleutnant Martin Pöppel, Company Commander in Battalion of the Paratroop Army, reporting back after five years of war and one year in captivity in England.

GLOSSARY OF MILITARY RANKS USED IN THIS BOOK

(It must be remembered that exact parallels with British Army ranks are often not possible)

Jäger	Private
Gefreite	acting Lance Corporal
Obergefreite	Lance Corporal
Oberjäger	In the German paratroops, rank above Gefreite level, approximating to Corporal
Unteroffizier	Corporal, but with connotations of NCO
Feldwebel	Lance Sergeant
Oberfeldwebel	Sergeant
Hauptfeldwebel	Staff Sergeant
Fahnenjunker (Feldwebel)	Officer Candidate (with rank of Sergeant)
Fähnrich	Officer Candidate, rank above Fahnenjunker but not yet an officer
Leutnant	Second Lieutenant
Oberleutnant	Lieutenant
Hauptmann	Captain
Major	Major
Oberstleutnant	Lieutenant Colonel
Oberst	Colonel
Generalleutnant	Lieutenant General
Generalmajor	Major General
General	General
Generalfeldmarschall	Field Marshal
Oberarzt	Army Doctor with rank of Lieutenant
Stabsarzt	Army Doctor with rank of Captain